Antonietta's

Classic Recipes

By

Antonietta Terrigno

Osteria de Medici
RISTORANTE

Canadian Cataloguing in Publication Data

Terrigno, Antonietta

Antonietta's Classic Recipes

Includes index.

ISBN 0-921146-28-0. 2nd revised edition, 1999 (ISBN 0-921146-08-6. 1st edition, 1995).

I. Cookery, Italian

I. Title. II. Title: Classic Recipes

TX723.T37 1999   641.5945   C99-910965-0

Osteria de Medici

201 - 10th Street NW

Calgary, Alberta T2N 1V5

Phone (403) 283-5553

Printed and bound in Canada

This book is dedicated to my children

Maurizio and Michael

and my husband

Rocco

Foreward

This book is the result of many years of experience, love of cooking, and caring about peoples' nutrition.

Indeed, I learned the very first rudiments of cooking from my grandmother Luisa and my mother Giovanna. Both were always very busy in the kitchen. At that time, every single dish was prepared from scratch (pasta, sauces, salami, prosciutto, cheese, bread, etc.). Assisting my elders in taking care of my brothers and sisters, I developed pride in the quality of the meals that I serve. This is definitely a trait portrayed in our restaurant "Osteria de Medici", and every guest must be completely satisfied with their meals, both in presentation and in taste.

Over the years learning and refining techniques that were handed down through generations and through travelling throughout Europe discovering new ideas, I have come to love preparing good food for people and most of all, enjoying their company while they sit back and relax for a wonderful dining experience. Italian cuisine is widely recognized to be the most genuine and the healthiest; fresh and savory produce makes it possible to prepare tasty and exquisite dishes. Olive oil is considered to be helpful in reducing cholesterol. Artichokes are very beneficial to the vital functions of the liver. Swisschard, asparagus, squash, zucchini, eggplant, tomatoes, etc. are excellent ingredients to prepare delicious soups, sauces and salads.

I have decided to make public my long standing experience by publishing a few recipes and share some advice that will be appreciated by all who have come to appreciate Italian cuisine.

In this day and age, it is important to be able to quickly prepare good nutritious meals, that is why each one of the recipes that are in this book indicate the preparation time and the cooking time, allowing you to choose recipes that fit into your schedule.

I hope you will enjoy preparing these wonderful recipes for your family and friends as much as I do.

To Your Health!

Buona Fortuna!

Antonietta Terrigno

Contents

Olives

Osteria de Medici
RISTORANTE

THE INGREDIENTS OF GREAT

ITALIAN COOKING

Broth

Olive Oil

Prosciutto

Rice

Tomatoes

Cheese

Herbs

Wine

Osteria de Medici

RISTORANTE

The Ingredients of Great Italian Cooking

Broth

Good broth is not only nourishing, but also an important element in Italian cooking. It is also vital to risotto and to innumerable soups. You will find a recipe for Meat Broth which is made with several cuts of top quality meats.

Olive Oils

Olive oil should have the greenish colour and fragrance of olives. It comes in three basic grades:

Extra Virgin Oil, made from olives that are not quite ripe, and is produced by stone crushing and cold pressing. Because it is produced without chemicals, it is of the highest quality and the most flavourful oil.

Virgin Olive Oil, is produced the same way as extra virgin olive oil, but is made from riper olives.

Pure Olive Oil, is the most common grade. It is produced by chemical means and contains only olive oils, without the blending of seed oil, hence the name "pure". Most brands available in supermarkets are usually "pure olive oil".

Prosciutto

Prosciutto is nonsmoked, salted and air-cured ham. It is widely used in Italian cooking, as well as served as an appetizer with ripe figs or cantaloupe.

Rice

Italian rice (**Riso**) is short and thick grained. It is the perfect rice for the delicious and unique preparation of risotto. Years ago it was impossible to find Italian rice in Calgary likewise in most other parts of Canada. Today the best and most widely exported grain from Italy is Arborio – to achieve the perfect risotto, Arborio is your best choice.

Tomatoes

To prepare the perfect sauce, you need good quality tomatoes. The best tomatoes are grown in the southern regions of Italy.

Cheese

Parmesan Cheese, or more correctly **Parmigiano Reggiano**, is from a group of Italian cheeses known collectively as **formaggi di grana**, meaning hard cheeses with a grainy texture. The cheeses are matured for two to three years and are categorized as vecchio (old), stravecchio (extra old), tipico (four or five years old), or giovane (less mature table cheeses). Parmesan should always be grated, never shredded.

Mozzarella, originally made from buffalo's milk, Mozzarella is now made from cow's milk. It is widely available in grocery stores but for the best quality check your local Italian grocer.

Herbs

Basil, is one of the most popular herbs and is commonly used in Italian cooking. Fresh basil can be cut up or chopped and kept in olive oil, ready to use whenever needed in soups, salads, sauces and in preparing meat and fish.

Rosemary, is an aromatic herb that is excellent for roasted meats, marinades and savory breads.

Oregano, fresh oregano is mild, sweet and aromatic and is excellent in fresh tomato sauces. Use dry oregano in moderation.

Garlic, is the most widely used root herb in the world and is a major ingredient in all Italian cooking. Garlic is not usually used alone but works along with other ingredients to add a flavourful taste to a variety of foods.

Wine

Wine, good enough for cooking, should also be good enough to drink. Every ingredient you put into a dish affects its quality – wine is no exception. Using a little bit of good wine will improve the quality of your dish and your mood, as you will probably be sipping a little bit as you cook.

Marsala Wine

This wonderful aromatic wine comes from Marsala, Sicily. Most Italian families have a standard supply of Marsala wine in their pantry. Marsala comes sweet and dry. Always use sweet Marsala for cooking; of the imported brands, Florio and Pellegrino, both produced in Marsala, are the best. Domestic Marsala should be used if nothing else is available.

Tomato Plants

Sauces are the base ingredients to Italian cooking.

The following sauce recipes are the foundation for the recipes in this cook book.

Tomato Sauce

Makes 2 litres

Preparation Time: 20 minutes
Cooking Time: 2 – 3 hours

1/2 cup	olive oil
1	medium onion, diced
1	medium green onion, diced
4	garlic cloves, minced
2 tbsps	salt
1 tsp	oregano
1 tbsp	black pepper
3 cups	water
1 tbsp	fresh parsley, minced
2.8 kgs	canned crushed tomatoes

Warm olive oil in large skillet, add onion, pepper, and garlic. Fry for 5 minutes and add the rest of the ingredients. Cook for 2 hours at a low temperature, stirring occasionally.

Sauce is ready to serve with any seafood, pasta or veal dish.

Comments:

Demi-Glace

2 litres	canned beef consomme or broth
1/2 lb	butter
1/2 lb	all purpose flour
1	medium onion
1	carrot
1	celery stalk
4	bay leaves
3	garlic cloves
1 tsp	black pepper corns
1	small can tomato paste

In a large pot melt butter and add the flour. Mix thoroughly. Add remaining ingredients and bring to a boil. Reduce heat and simmer for 2 hours. Strain and use in sauces as is.

Comments:

Besciamella Sauce

(WHITE SAUCE)

Makes 2 cups

Preparation Time: 5 minutes
Cooking Time: 1/2 hour

1/2 litre	milk
1/4 lb	butter
1/2 cup	flour
pinch	salt and pepper
1/2 tsp	nutmeg

Heat milk in a saucepot until it is very close to the boiling point. Set aside. In another saucepot melt butter on medium heat. When the butter has reached the frothing point add flour, salt and pepper, and nutmeg. Stir well. Add hot milk slowly stirring with a wire whisk or a wooden spoon (stir in the same direction). To prevent lumps from forming lower the heat and let sauce cook for 15 minutes, stirring frequently.

Comments:

Meat Sauce

Makes 2 litres

Preparation Time: 15 minutes
Cooking Time: 1 hour

100 grams	ground beef
200 grams	ground pork
200 grams	ground veal
1	green pepper, medium diced
1	onion, medium diced
1	celery stick, diced
4	garlic cloves, minced
1 tbsp	salt
1 tsp	pepper
1/2 cup	olive oil
3 cups	chicken broth
2 litres	canned tomatoes

Saute vegetables and garlic for 3 minutes. Add the meat and cook for an additional 15 minutes. Add tomatoes, broth, salt and pepper. Simmer for at least two hours. Stir occasionally.

Comments:

Brodo Di Pollo

(CHICKEN BROTH)

Makes 2 – 3 litres

Preparation Time: 15 minutes
Cooking Time: 2 1/2 hours

1 lb	chicken
2	celery stalks
1	medium onion
1	large carrot
	salt and pepper to taste
5 litres	water

Cut chicken in half. In a large sauce pot place the chicken, celery, onion, carrot, salt and pepper along with the water. Bring to a boil; reduce heat and simmer for 2 hours. Remove the froth from the top with a slotted spoon. Remove the chicken from the pot and reserve for use in other dishes. Strain the broth through a fine sieve. Cool and chill in the refrigerator. Keep refrigerated or freeze in small containers. Broth will keep in the refrigerator for up to 5 days.

Comments:

Bernaise Sauce

(TERRAGON BUTTER SAUCE)

Makes 1/2 litre

Preparation Time: 5 minutes
Cooking Time: 5 minutes

1/2 lbs	butter
4	egg yolks
1/4 cup	white wine
1 tbsp	tarragon
1	juice of a lemon
pinch	tabasco
pinch	worcestershire sauce
	salt and pepper (to taste)

Melt butter in a small sauce pan and set aside over a double boiler whisk together eggs and white wine until mixture becomes fairly thick, but not scrambled eggs. Remove from heat and let sit for about 1 min. Slowly whisk in a little butter at a time, then add remaining ingredients.

Comments:

Beurre Manier

1/4 lb   soft butter
1/4 lb   all purpose flour

Mix butter and flour together till fully mixed. Use beurre manier to thicken soups and sauces. Use a little at a time till it thickens. This mix can be stored in a fridge for long period of time.

Comments:

Firenze
(Florence, Italy)

Osteria de Medici
RISTORANTE

Pastella

(BATTER)

Makes 2 cups

Preparation Time: 5 minutes
Cooking Time: 5 – 10 minutes

4	whole eggs
1 tbsp	baking powder
	flour
	salt and pepper (to taste)

Mix eggs and baking powder together and add a little at a time till it becomes fairly thick. Make sure the batter is smooth, then add salt and pepper. Heat oil in a deep fryer. Dip desired item in the batter and fry till golden brown.

Comments:

Appetizers

The antipasto course, which precedes the first course, has been part of festive Italian meals since as early as the sixteenth century. Its components vary greatly depending on where you are in Molise and whether you are eating in a home or a restaurant. The antipasto course may consist of a mixed platter of local preserved meats and crostini or, for a special dinner prepared at home, it may be a single elaborate hot or cold dish.

Bruschetta

Serves 6 – 10 people

Preparation Time: 15 minutes
Cooking Time: 5 minutes

Part A: Topping

10	medium tomatoes, diced into small pieces
1 tsp	black pepper
1 tsp	salt
1 tbsp	oregano
4	garlic cloves, minced
1/2 cup	olive oil

Mix all ingredients together in a bowl and refrigerate overnight.

Part B: Bread

10	Italian dinner rolls, cut in half
1/4 lb	soft butter
4	shallots, chopped fine

Combine butter and shallots. Spread mixture on bread and place on a baking sheet, toast till brown. Spoon topping onto heated bread and serve.

Comments:

Garlic Crostini

Makes 32 Crostini

Preparation Time: 5 minutes
Baking Time: 10 minutes

1/4 cup	100% pure olive oil
2	garlic cloves, minced
1	baguette, cut in 1 inch slices

Preheat oven to 375 F. Combine oil and garlic in a small bowl. Place baguette slices on a baking sheet. Brush the tops of the slices with oil and garlic mixture. Bake 10 minutes or until lightly toasted. Serve with dips and spreads.

Comments:

Mushroom Grissini

Serves 8 people

1 tbsp	olive oil
1	fresh clove garlic, crushed
4 cups	mushrooms, sliced
1 tsp	salt
1 tsp	pepper
1 cup	whipping cream
2 oz	brandy
8 slices	toast

Sauté garlic in oil. Add sliced mushrooms and whipping cream. Reduce heat and stir until thickened, place on toast and serve.

Comments:

Antipasto Frutti Di-Mare

(COLD SEAFOOD APPETIZER)

Serves 4 people

Preparation Time: 20 minutes
Cooking Time: 10 minutes

8	medium scallops
3 – 6	squid
8	shrimp
16	mussels
1 cup	red pepper, diced
1 cup	green pepper, diced
2 cups	olive oil
1/4 cup	red wine vinegar
1 tsp	each of oregano, salt, black pepper
1	fresh lemon
	fresh parsley

Boil all seafood in lemon juice and water for 5 minutes, drain and cool, season with salt and pepper. boil the red and green peppers in the vinegar for 10 minutes and cool. Add the remaining ingredients. Spoon pepper mixture over seafood, garnish with fresh parsley and lemons.

Comments:

Escargot

Lumache All'anice

(SNAILS WITH ANISE)

Serves 6 people

Preparation Time: 10 minutes
Cooking Time: 10 minutes

3	garlic cloves, minced
1	pearl onion, chopped fine
2 tbsp	fresh parsley, chopped fine
3/4 cup	butter, softened
3 oz	anisette liqueur
36	snails

Preheat oven to 400 F. Prepare anise butter by mixing the first five ingredients together. Put snails on snail plates and cover each snail with anise butter. Bake for 10 minutes or until the butter is bubbling. Serve immediately.

Comments:

Prosciutto Con Melone

Prosciutto Con Melone

(PROSCIUTTO WITH MELON)

Serves 4 people   *Preparation Time: 5 minutes*

2	cantaloupes
12	thin slices of prosciutto

Peel and slice the cantaloupes into 12 slices. Place three slices of cantaloupe per plate and lay a slice of prosciutto on each.

Comments:

Antipasto Di Gamberetti

(SHRIMP COCKTAIL)

Serves 6 people

Preparation Time: 15 minutes

Cooking Time: 5 minutes

30	fresh large shrimp, peeled and deveined
6 cups	water
1	lemon, squeeze for juice
2 cups	ketchup
1/2 cup	brandy
2 tbsp	horseradish
2 tsp	salt
1 tsp	pepper
1 1/2 cups	shredded lettuce

Bring water to a boil. Add salt and half of the lemon juice. Add shrimp and cook over medium heat till the flesh turns completely white. Drain and let cool. Mix together the ketchup, brandy, horseradish, salt and pepper. When ready to serve place lettuce on the bottom of a champagne glass, top with sauce and hang shrimp over the rim of the glass.

Comments:

32

Calamari Fritti

(DEEP FRIED SQUID)

Serves 4 – 6 people

2 1/2 lb	fresh squid
1 cup	flour
2 cups	oil
	lemon wedges

Slice body crosswise into 3/4 inch-thick slices. Cut tentacles if they are large. Dry off squid and lightly flour. In a large skillet heat oil until it is very hot. Carefully add squid turning on both sides. Cook until the squid is crispy. Sprinkle with salt and garnish with lemon wedges.

*if you over cook the squid they will be too tough to eat, squid should be slightly raw in the middle

Comments:

Fine Dining

Osteria de Medici
RISTORANTE

(403) 283-5553

CATHERINE DE' MEDICI
(1519 - 1589)

When she was only 14 Catherine went to France to marry the future King Henry II. She brought with her, besides refined manners, many of the delicacies that were then enjoyed in Renaissance Italy: sweetbreads, truffles, artichoke hearts, quenelles of poultry, ice cream and frangipane tarts.

Osteria de Medici
RISTORANTE

Salads

1. When washing lettuce, squeeze the juice of 1 or 2 lemons into the water and also add about 1/2 tsp. salt. The lemon juice adds to the crispness of the lettuce and the salt will drive out any insects hidden in the lettuce leaves.

2. If lettuce seems to be limp, add ice cubes to the water and allow lettuce to soak a few minutes.

3. After thorough washing, dry lettuce thoroughly between towels or drain well in a salad basket.

4. Always chill lettuce after it is cleaned. Put in a cloth bag or other closed container in refrigerator to keep cold and crispy.

5. If you wish tomatoes to be added to a salad, prepare them separately and use them as garnish. If they are added along with the other ingredients, their juice will thin the dressing.

6. It is best to cut tomatoes in vertical slices because they bleed less this way.

7. A tastier tossed salad will result if several kinds of lettuce are used.

8. Always taste a tossed salad before serving. If it seems dull, add a little more vinegar or salt and pepper.

9. Chill salad plates (bowls), especially if serving individual salads.

10. For a change of pace, try chilling the salad forks, too. You'll be amazed at the reactions you'll receive.

Insalata Di Zucchini

(MARINATED ZUCCHINI SALAD)

Serves 6 people

Preparation Time: 20 minutes
Chilling Time: 2 hours

2 small	zucchinis, cleaned and cubed
3 med	tomatoes, chopped
1 small	red onion, chopped
2 tbsp	fresh basil, chopped
1 tbsp	olive oil
2 tbsp	balsamic vinegar
1/2 tsp	fresh ground pepper

Boil zucchini, and cool. In a non metal bowl, combine all ingredients. Refrigerate a minimum of 2 hours before serving.

Comments:

Insalata Di Vedure Miste

(MIXED SALAD)

Serves 6 people   *Preparation Time: 10 minutes*

1/2	head of butter leaf lettuce
1	small head of endive lettuce
2	tomatoes, quartered
1	celery stalk, sliced thick
2	fennel bulbs, sliced 1/2 inch thick
3	small radishes, sliced thin
	oil and vinegar
	salt to taste

Discard outer leaves from greens. Wash quickly and pat dry with towels. Tear into bite sized pieces and place in a large salad bowl. Slice celery, fennel, radishes, tomatoes and add to salad. Season with salt and add enough oil to coat ingredients. Sprinkle with vinegar and toss gently to mix.

Comments:

Caesar Salad

Serves 8 people

Preparation Time: 20 minutes

1	head of romaine
1 cup	croutons
5	cloves of garlic
1/2 cup	parmesan cheese
4	egg yolks
3	anchovy filets, chopped
1 tbsp.	capers, chopped
1 cup	olive oil
1/2 tsp	dry mustard
	pinch tabasco sauce
	pinch of worcestershire sauce
	salt and pepper to taste
2	lemons

Wash and cut romaine and store in a cloth towel. In a mixing bowl add egg yolk, garlic, capers, anchovy and mustard, mix on high with blender slowing to add oil till completely absorbed. Then add juice of lemons, tabasco, Worcestershire sauce and salt and pepper. Mix together lettuce, croutons, cheese, add dressing and mix together.

Comments:

Insalata Di Arance

(ORANGE SALAD)

Serves 4 – 6 people   *Preparation Time: 5 minutes*

6	oranges
1 tbsp	olive oil
1 tsp	salt
	pepper to taste

Peel oranges and slice into rounds. Add oil, salt, and freshly ground pepper.

Comments:

Insalata Di Arance

(ORANGE SALAD)

4	small bunches of Belgium endive
3	oranges
1 tbsp	french mustard (dijon)
1/2 cup	oil
1	lemon, squeezed for juice
	salt and pepper to taste

Discard outer leaves from the endive. Wash quickly and thoroughly in cold water and dry. Tear into bite-sized pieces and place into a large salad bowl. Peel and split oranges into sections and add to greens. Combine mustard, oil, lemon, salt and pepper. Mix well. Pour over salad and toss gently. Serve immediately.

Comments:

Insalata Di Pomodoro

(TOMATO SALAD)

Serves 6 people

6	ripe tomatoes
1	garlic clove, minced
1 tsp	oregano
6	fresh basil leaves
1/2 cup	olive oil
1/4 cup	red wine vinegar
	salt to taste

Wash the tomatoes and slice. Place slices on a platter in one layer. Sprinkle with salt, garlic, oregano and basil leaves. Pour olive oil over tomatoes and sprinkle with red wine vinegar. Let stand for about 10 minutes then serve.

Comments:

Insalata Di Peperoni

(ROASTED PEPPER SALAD)

Serves 4 – 6 people

Preparation Time: 15 minutes
Cooking Time: 30 minutes

6	large mixed peppers (green and red)
1	garlic clove, minced
1/4 cup	olive oil
	salt to taste

Preheat oven to 400 F. Lay whole peppers on the bottom of a baking dish and place in the oven for about 20 minutes. Turn peppers frequently so the skin will be evenly roasted (skin should blister). Remove from the oven and let cool for about 10 minutes. Peel and remove the stems and seeds. Cut the peppers into thin strips and place them in a serving dish. Add garlic and oil. Season with salt and mix well. Let stand for about an hour then serve.

Comments:

Insalata Di Fagiolini

(GREEN BEANS WITH TOMATOES)

Serves 4 people

Preparation Time: 20 minutes
Cooking Time: 20 minutes

1 lb	fresh green beans
2	fresh tomatoes, quartered
1/2 cup	olive oil
1	lemon, squeezed for juice
	salt and pepper to taste

Trim and cut beans into 1 inch pieces. Cook beans in boiling salted water until tender. Drain and cool. In a large bowl combine beans, tomatoes, oil, lemon juice, salt and pepper. Mix well.

Comments:

Insalata Di Bocconcini E Pomidoro

(FRESH CHEESE AND TOMATO SALAD)

Serves 6 people

6	medium tomatoes
6	bocconcini cheese
1 cup	olive oil
1/2 cup	balsamic vinegar
1 tsp	salt
1 tsp	pepper
1 tsp	oregano
1 tsp	parsley

Slice tomatoes and bocconcini cheese crosswise. In a bowl mix the other ingredients. Place tomato and cheese on plates and pour dressing over the top.

Comments:

Insalata Di Finocchio

(FENNEL SALAD)

Serves 6 people   *Preparation Time: 10 minutes*

4	heads of fennel, sliced
1/2 cup	olive oil
	salt and pepper to taste

Combine all ingredients in a large bowl and mix together well.

Comments:

Minestrone

1/3 cup	olive oil
1	large zucchini, diced
1	medium carrot, diced
1	medium onion, diced
8 pcs	celery, diced
3	peeled potatoes, diced
1/2 cup	prosciutto
1/2 cup	cooked spinach
2 cups	whole stewed tomatoes
8 cups	chicken broth
	salt and pepper to taste

Heat oil in a saucepot and saute the vegetables with the prosciutto for approximately 10 minutes. Add the stewed tomatoes and continue cooking for another 10 minutes. Add broth and cook till vegetables are soft, then add spinach and salt and pepper. Serve.

Comments:

Zuppa Di Pesce

(FISH SOUP)

Serves 10 – 12 people

Preparation Time: 45 minutes
Cooking Time: 4 hours

4 lbs	assorted fresh fish, cut in large pieces (conger, eel, perch, turbot, red mullet, scallops)
1 lb	assorted shellfish, leave in shell (clams, baby lobster, shrimps, mussels, crab legs)
1 cup	oil
28 oz	peeled tomatoes, chopped fine and save liquid
1	onion, chopped fine
1 leek	(heart only), chopped fine
1	garlic clove, minced
1 pinch	zafferano
1 tsp	thyme

Wash and clean all seafood. Place seafood in a large pot and add remaining ingredients except the wine, chicken broth and croutons. Mix well and let marinade for 2–3 hours stirring occasionally. Place the saucepan on the burner and cook for 15 minutes on high heat. Stir frequently. Pour wine and broth over the seafood and continue cooking for another 10 minutes. Reduce heat. Stir well. Remove from heat. Remove seafood and place on platter. In each soup bowl add croutons and pour broth over croutons. Serve soup together with fish.

Comments:

Zuppa Di Lenticchie

(LENTIL SOUP)

Serves 6 – 8 people

Preparation Time: 20 minutes
Cooking Time: 1 hour

Part A: Lentils

8 cups	water
1/2 lb	dried lentils
2	whole medium potatoes

Part B: Sauce

8 oz	plum style canned Italian Tomatoes
1	small onion, chopped fine
1	small carrot, chopped fine
1	celery stalk, chopped fine
1	garlic clove, minced
2	strips bacon, chopped fine
2 tbsp	oil
1 tsp	butter

Soak lentils in cold water overnight or for at least 6 hours. Drain and place in a saucepan with potatoes and cover with water. Bring to a boil, reduce heat and cook until lentils are tender. Drain and save liquid.

In another saucepan saute onion, celery, garlic, and bacon in oil and butter. Then add peeled tomatoes and the liquid. Simmer for half an hour. Remove potatoes from lentils and mash. Return to lentil pot and cover with the sauce. Add salt and pepper. Bring to a boil and simmer for 5 minutes. Remove from heat and serve.

Comments:

Zuppa Di Zucchini Con Riso

(ZUCCHINI AND RICE SOUP)

Serves 4 people

Preparation Time: 30 minutes
Cooking Time: 1 hour

1	small onion, chopped fine
1	garlic clove, minced
1 tbsp	butter
3 tbsp	oil
2	medium fresh tomatoes
3	zucchini, diced large
8 cups	chicken broth
1 1/2 cups	rice, uncooked
	salt and pepper to taste

In a large saucepan, saute onion and garlic in oil and butter. Add zucchini and tomatoes, mixing well. Simmer for 3/4 of an hour. Add broth, one chicken cube, rice, salt, and pepper. Bring to a boil. Reduce heat and simmer until rice is tender, stirring frequently. Sprinkle with grated parmesan cheese and serve.

Comments:

Crema Di Pollo

(CREAM OF CHICKEN SOUP)

Serves 6 people

Preparation Time: 15 minutes
Cooking Time: 2 1/2 hours

1 lb	chicken
2	celery stalks
1	medium onion
1	large carrot, peeled
4 1/2	quarts water
1 cup	butter
1 cup	flour
2	egg yolks
2 oz	whipping cream
	salt and pepper to taste

Cut chicken in half and place in a stock pot together with celery, onion, carrot, salt and pepper, and water. Bring to a boil. Reduce heat and simmer for 2 hours, occasionally skimming the froth from the top. Remove chicken, debone and chop finely. Set aside. Strain and reserve broth. Melt butter in a large saucepan over medium heat. Gradually add flour, stirring well. Add 2 quarts chicken broth and simmer over low heat for about half an hour, stirring occasionally. Remove from heat and add chicken pieces, egg yolks and whipping cream stirring well for about 5 minutes. Serve immediately.

Comments:

Zuppa Pavese

(POACHED EGGS IN BROTH)

Serves 4 people

Preparation Time: 5 minutes
Cooking Time: 5 minutes

6 cups	chicken broth
4	eggs
1 cup	croutons
4 tbsp	grated parmesan cheese

In a medium saucepan bring chicken broth to a boil. Reduce heat and simmer. Carefully break one egg into each soup bowl and top with croutons and one tablespoon of parmesan cheese. Pour a cup of broth over each egg and serve immediately.

Comments:

Zuppa Di Spinaci

(SPINACH SOUP)

Serves 6 people

Preparation Time: 15 minutes
Cooking Time: 45 minutes

2 lbs	fresh spinach
8 cups	chicken broth
2	garlic cloves, minced
1/2 cup	parmesan cheese, grated
4 cups	water
	salt and pepper to taste

Wash spinach and remove stems, place in a saucepot with water and simmer until just limp. Drain and chop fine. Set aside. In a large saucepot add chicken broth, garlic, salt, pepper, and cooked spinach. Bring to a boil. Reduce heat and add parmesan cheese. Simmer for 1/2 hour and remove from heat.

Comments:

Stracciatella Alla Romana

(CHICKEN SOUP WITH EGG)

Serves 4 people

Preparation Time: 5 minutes
Cooking Time: 5 minutes

3	eggs, beaten
1/2 cup	grated parmesan cheese
1 tbsp	fresh parsley, chopped finely
4 cups	chicken broth

In a small bowl beat eggs, parmesan cheese and parsley. Mix well and set aside. In a medium saucepan bring chicken broth to a boil on high heat. Add egg mixture. Simmer for 5 minutes (do not stir). Remove from heat and divide soup evenly.

Comments:

Capellini In Brodo

(ANGEL HAIR WITH BROTH)

Serves 6 people

Preparation Time: 5 minutes
Cooking Time: 10 minutes

3 litres	chicken broth
500 g	angle hair pasta
	salt and pepper

Cook Angel hair in an abundance of salted boiling water for approx. 3-5 minutes. Meanwhile bring broth to a boil and season with salt and pepper; strain pasta and add it to the broth and ladle into bowls.

Comments:

Zuppa Di Scarola

(CURLY ENDIVE SOUP)

Serves 6 people

Preparation Time: 10 minutes
Cooking Time: 30 minutes

3	heads of endive
3 litres	chicken broth
1 tsp	salt
1 tsp	black ground pepper
3	garlic cloves, minced
3 tsp	parsley, chopped

Cook endives in salted boiling water for approximately 10 minutes. Drain water and chop endive and add to the broth with the garlic, salt, pepper and parsley and simmer for one half hour.

Comments:

Piazza Roma

Pasta E Fagioli

Pasta E Fagioli

(ITALIAN BEAN SOUP)

Serves 8 people

Preparation Time: 45 minutes
Cooking Time: 3 hours

1 lb	chopped prosciutto
4 cups	dried bean (white or brown)
1	medium carrot, diced
1	medium onion, diced
1	large green pepper, diced
16 cups	chicken broth
1 tsp	dried rosemary
1 tsp	sage
3	garlic cloves, minced
3 cups	whole stewed tomatoes
2 cups	macaroni
	salt and pepper to taste

Soak beans in water overnight and strain. Saute vegetables in a large saucepan with the prosciutto and chicken broth. Cook till beans become soft and soup thickens. In a small saucepan brown garlic, rosemary and sage. Add this to the soup. Add cooked pasta, season with salt and pepper.

Comments:

efore Marco Polo went to the valley "Del Katai", pasta was already created; instead of spaghetti it was then called rishta, an Arabic word. When Marco Polo returned to Venezia, Italy in the 13th century he brought with him wheat flour. It was used to make spaghetti and bread. The pasta was prepared on a large wooden table, mixed by hand, and hydrated with underground well water. To make pasta thin, wooden tubes were used to wrap the mixture around thus creating the thin pieces of pasta. Different styles of pasta were developed, cutting it shorter for the use in tomato soup; a favorite of the princes and princesses. The Medici family taught the people how to cook pasta and how to eat pasta with a fork and spoon. I am proud to introduce to the entire world pasta with sauce, which in Italian is called, "La Pastasciuttas".

Cooking Pasta

Knowing how to cook pasta is very important in Italian cuisine to cook pasta you need a generous amount of salted water. A good rule to know is about 4 times the amount of water to pasta. For example, for 500 grams of penne you would need 2 litres of water and 1 tbsp of salt per litre. Make sure the water comes to a boil before adding the pasta, and always stir the pasta to prevent it from sticking together. To tell when pasta is done it should be soft and slightly firm to the bite. Then strain the pasta and serve with the desired dish.

Spaghetti Al Forno

(BAKED SPAGHETTI)

Serves 4 – 6 people

Preparation Time: 20 minutes
Cooking Time: 10 minutes

10 oz	cooked spaghetti
1 tsp	dried basil or thyme
1 lb	lean ground beef
1	clove crushed garlic
1 tsp	oregano leaves or Italian spice
1	onion chopped
2 cups	spaghetti sauce
1/4 cup	chopped green pepper
1 cup	shredded mozzarella cheese
	salt and pepper to taste

Toss 4 cups cooked spaghetti with basil or thyme and place in the bottom and up the sides of a 10" glass pie plate. Meanwhile, brown ground beef with garlic, oregano, onion and ground pepper. Drain off any excess fat. Add spaghetti sauce, green pepper. Simmer for 2–3 minutes. Pour into centre of pie plate. Garnish with additional ground beef if desired. Cover loosely and heat in oven for 5 minutes. Top with cheese. Let stand covered for 5 minutes before serving. Cut into wedges and serve with tossed salad.

Comments:

Spaghetti Con Mozzarella & Tomatoes

Makes 4 servings

Preparation Time: 10 minutes
Cooking Time: 10 minutes
Marinating Time: 10 minutes

3	tomatoes, cut into cubes
1 1/2 cups	cubed mozzarella cheese
2	garlic cloves, minced
1/2 cup	packed fresh basil leaves, finely chopped
1 tsp	pepper
1/2 tsp	salt
2	green onions, finely chopped
1/4 cup	100% pure virgin olive oil
3/4 lb	spaghetti

In a large bowl, stir together tomatoes, mozzarella cubes, garlic, basil, pepper, salt and green onions. Drizzle with oil and toss to combine. Let stand 30 minutes. Meanwhile, in a large pot of boiling, salted water, cook pasta 8–10 minutes, or until tender but firm. Drain and toss immediately with marinated tomato mixture. Serve with freshly ground black pepper.

Comments:

Pasta Con Tonno e Olive

(PASTA WITH TUNA & OLIVES)

Makes 6 servings

Preparation Time: 10 minutes
Cooking Time: 20 minutes

2 tbsp	100% pure olive oil
2	garlic cloves, minced
1 can	(28 oz) tomatoes
1/2 tsp	each dried oregano, salt and pepper
1/4 tsp	hot pepper flakes
1 lb	bucatini
1 cup	sliced medium pitted black olives
1/4 cup	chopped fresh parsley
2 cans	(7 oz) solid light tuna, drained and separated into pieces

In a saucepan, heat oil over medium heat. Add garlic and cook 10 seconds, or until golden brown. Add tomatoes, oregano, salt, pepper and hot pepper flakes; bring to a boil. Reduce heat to medium–low and cook 15 minutes. Meanwhile, in a pot of boiling, salted water, cook pasta 8–10 minutes, or until tender but firm. Drain well. Stir olives into sauce and cook 2 minutes. Toss pasta with sauce, parsley and tuna. Serve immediately.

Comments:

Linguini Alla Puttanesca

Makes 4 servings

Preparation Time: 10 minutes
Cooking Time: 25 minutes

1 can	(28 oz) tomatoes
2 tbsp	100% pure virgin olive oil
2 cans	anchovy fillets, drained and finely chopped (optional)
4	garlic cloves, minced
1/2 cup	each sliced, pitted medium ripe olives and sliced Primo stuffed manzanilla olives
2 tbsp	drained capers
1/2 tsp	hot pepper flakes
1/4 tsp	each dried oregano and salt
3/4 lb	linguini
1/4 cup	chopped fresh Italian parsley

Place tomatoes and juice in food processor. Pulse on and off until tomatoes are crushed; set aside. In large skillet, heat olive oil over medium heat. Add anchovies (if using), garlic, olives, capers, hot pepper flakes, oregano and salt. Cook 3 minutes or until garlic softens, stirring constantly. Stir in tomatoes; cook 20 minutes or until sauce thickens. Meanwhile, in a pot of boiling, salted water, cook pasta 6 minutes, or until tender but firm. Drain well. Toss with sauce and fresh parsley. Serve immediately.

Comments:

Seafood Lasagna

Makes 12 servings

2	Primo lasagna noodles
1	(475 g) container light ricotta
1/2 cup	100% grated parmesan cheese
1/3 cup	table cream (18% mf)
1/2 cup	butter
2 cups	chopped fennel
1	onion, chopped
1/2 cup	all purpose flour
4 cups	milk
1 lb	cooked seafood (shrimp, scallops, lobster, clams or mussels)
1 cup	shredded mozzarella cheese

In a large pot of salted, boiling water, cook lasagna noodles 10–12 minutes or until tender. Rinse under cold water, drain and set aside. In a bowl, stir together ricotta, parmesan and cream; set aside. In a large, heavy bottomed saucepan melt butter over medium heat. Add fennel and onion; reduce heat to medium-low, and cook 10 minutes, or until softened. Add flour and cook 1 minute, stirring constantly. Gradually add milk, whisking constantly. Bring mixture to a boil over medium heat, stirring constantly. Reduce heat to low and simmer 10 minutes or until thickened, stirring occasionally. Remove 1 cup of sauce and set aside. Add seafood to simmering sauce and cook 30 seconds, or until seafood is slightly warmed, stirring constantly. Spread 1/4 cup of reserved white sauce in bottom of a 13 x 9 inch baking dish. Layer with three lasagna noodles. Spoon half of the seafood sauce on top of noodles. Layer with three more lasagna noodles. Spoon remaining seafood sauce on top and cover with last three lasagna noodles. Pour remaining 3/4 cup of reserved white sauce on top, sprinkle with mozzarella. Bake at 350 F for 25 minutes, or until heated through and mozzarella is melted.

Comments:

Gnocchi Alla Romana

(DUMPLINGS ROMAN STYLE)

Serves 8 people

Preparation Time: 5 minutes
Cooking Time: 1 hour

4 cups	milk
300 gr	coarse semolina
1 tbsp	olive oil
1 tbsp	butter
3	egg yolks
	parmesan cheese
	salt and pepper to taste

Bring milk to a boil and whisk in semolina. Add butter and oil. Let cook for 30 minutes on low. Add cheese and egg yolks, then spread on oiled baking sheet one inch thick and cool in refrigerator. Cut into circles with a cup. Place butter in a baking dish place gnocchi on top and sprinkle with cheese and bake at 350 F for 20 minutes.

Comments:

Bucatini Alla Rafrano

(PASTA WITH HORSERADISH)

Serves 6 people

Preparation Time: 10 minutes
Cooking Time: 10 minutes

500 gr	bucatini
2	garlic cloves crushed
1/4 cup	grated fresh horseradish
1/4 cup	bread crumbs
1/4 cup	butter
1/4 cup	parmesan cheese

Cook pasta in boiling salted water. Meanwhile melt butter in a saucepan and saute garlic. Strain pasta and add it to the pan, stir in remaining ingredients and serve. Remember this pasta has no sauce and is very dry.

Comments:

Spaghetti Con Funghi E Prosciutto

(SPAGHETTI WITH HAM AND ZUCCHINI)

Serves 4 people

Preparation Time: 10 minutes
Cooking Time: 20 minutes

2 cups	stewed tomatoes
1/2 cup	tomato paste
3/4 cup	cooked ham, slivered
1 med.	zucchini, quartered lengthwise and thinly sliced
1/2 cup	milk
1/2 cup	parmesan cheese
2 cups	mushroom

Combine tomatoes, tomato paste, ham, zucchini and mushroom in saucepan. Bring just to a boil, reduce heat and simmer for 5 minutes. Stir in milk and 1/4 cup of cheese, heat thoroughly. Serve over cooked pasta. Sprinkle with remaining cheese.

Comments:

Lasagne

Serves 6 people

Preparation Time: 30 minutes
Cooking Time: 1/2 – 1 hour

Part A: Pasta Dough Ingredients

6	whole eggs
2 kg	all purpose flour

Mix egg and flour together till it forms a nice smooth dough. Let stand for 2 hours. Using a pasta machine, roll out about 10 sheets at 8 inches long and cook them in boiling water and cool. If using dry pasta use the same process.

Part B: Mix Ingredients

2 litres	meat sauce
1 1/2 lbs	grated mozzarella cheese
2 cups	grated parmesan cheese

In a casserole place a little meat sauce on the bottom, then place two or three sheets of boiled pasta on the top. Pour a little more meat sauce and place grated mozzarella cheese and parmesan cheese on top. Repeat this process till it reaches the top of the pan and finish with the cheese on top. Bake at 350 F 30 – 40 minutes.

Comments:

Lasagne Roll-Ups

Serves 4 – 6 people

Preparation Time: 30 minutes
Cooking Time: 30 minutes

1 lb	Italian sausage meat
1/2 cup	chopped onion
1	garlic clove, crushed
1 1/3 cup	tomato paste
1 2/3 cup	water
1 tsp	oregano
1/2 tsp	basil
1 pkg	frozen chopped spinach (thawed and drained well)
2 cups	ricotta cheese
1 cup	parmesan cheese
1 1/2 cup	mozzarella cheese
1	egg slightly beaten
1/2 tsp	salt
1/4 tsp	pepper

Remove sausage from casings, crumble and brown sausage, onion and garlic in saucepan. Pour off excess fat. Add tomato paste, water, oregano and basil. Cover; boil sauce gently for 20 minutes. In medium bowl, combine spinach, ricotta cheese, parmesan cheese, 1 cup mozzarella cheese, egg, salt and pepper and mix well. Spread about 1/2 cup cheese mixture on each boiled noodle, roll up. Place seam side down in 12 x 8 inch baking dish, pour sauce over rolls. Top with remaining 1/2 cup mozzarella cheese. Bake at 350 F for 30 minutes, or until heated through.

Comments:

Rigatoni Al Forno

Rigatoni Al Forno

(BAKED RIGATONI)

Serves 4 people

Preparation Time: 20 minutes
Cooking Time: 5 minutes

500 grams	rigatoni
1 cup	grated parmigiano cheese
500 grams	grated mozzarella cheese
2 litres	meat sauce
8	mozzarella cheese slices

Cook pasta as directed and strain. Heat meat sauce and mix in with the pasta and the grated Mozzarella and Parmesan cheese. Place in a casserole. Place the sliced cheese on top and cook for 5 minutes at 450 F until the top is brown.

Comments:

Fusilli Principessa

(FUSILLI WITH ASPARAGUS)

Serves 4 people

Preparation Time: 10 minutes
Cooking Time: 15 minutes

500 grams	fusilli
2 cups	chopped asparagus tips
1 cup	sliced mushrooms
1/4 cup	brandy
1/2 litre	cream
1/2 cup	grated parmesan cheese
	salt and pepper to taste

In a saucepan saute mushrooms and asparagus. Add brandy and cream. Reduce heat until sauce starts to thicken. Add salt and pepper. Add cooked pasta and mix. Add parmesan cheese and mix.

Comments:

Capellini Alla Marinara

(ANGEL HAIR PASTA AND TOMATOES)

Serves 4 people

Preparation Time: 5 minutes
Cooking Time: 15 minutes

500 grams	capellini, (angel hair)
2	garlic cloves, minced
1/2	medium onion, diced
1 tsp	parsley, chopped
1 tsp	oregano
2	anchovy filets
1 litre	tomato sauce
1/2 cup	grated parmesan cheese
	salt and pepper to taste

Crush garlic and anchovy together till a paste forms. Saute onions and garlic/anchovy paste together. Then add oregano and parsley, followed by the tomato sauce. Cook for 5 minutes at medium heat. Meanwhile cook the pasta as directed. Strain the pasta and add to the sauce. Add cheese.

Comments:

Spaghetti Aglio E Olio

(SPAGHETTI IN GARLIC AND OIL)

Serves 4 people

Preparation Time: 10 minutes
Cooking Time: 10 minutes

1 lb	thin spaghetti or linguine
6	garlic cloves, minced
1/3 to 1/2 cup	extra virgin olive oil
	salt and freshly ground pepper to taste
1/2 cup	freshly grated parmesan cheese

Cook the pasta in an abundance of boiling, salted water. While pasta is cooking, heat the garlic in 1/3 cup oil in a frying pan over low heat. When the mixture just begins to bubble, stir and cook for a few more minutes until garlic just begins to turn golden. Do not let garlic brown. When pasta is partially cooked, drain it, add it to the frying pan and toss well. Season to taste with salt and pepper. Add a bit more oil if you like. Serve immediately with parmesan cheese.

Comments:

Penne All' Arrabbiata

(PENNE WITH SPICY TOMATO SAUCE)

Serves 6 people

Preparation Time: 10 minutes
Cooking Time: 15 minutes

2 lb	penne
1/2 cup	olive oil
2	garlic cloves, crushed
1 tsp	crushed chilies
3	ripe tomatoes, peeled and diced into large pieces
1/2 cup	grated parmesan cheese

Cook the pasta in an abundance of boiling, salted water. While pasta is cooking, heat the oil in a frying pan over medium heat. Add garlic and chilies and cook until garlic is golden in color and add tomatoes. Reduce heat and continue to cook for 10 to 15 minutes, stirring frequently. When pasta is partially cooked, drain it, add it to the frying pan and toss well. Season to taste with salt and pepper and add a bit more oil if you like. Serve immediately with Parmesan cheese.

Comments:

Baked Macaroni

Serves 6 people

Preparation Time: 10 minutes
Cooking Time: 30 minutes

1 lb — large elbow macaroni
1/4 cup — butter
1/2 cup — grated parmesan cheese
2 cups — besciamella sauce

Preheat oven to 350 F. Cook the pasta in an abundance of boiling, salted water. When pasta is partially cooked, drain and return to pot. Mix in butter and parmesan cheese, place in a casserole dish and cover with besciamella sauce. Bake for 1/2 an hour or until top is golden brown and crispy.

Comments:

Linguini Con Capesante

(LINGUINI WITH SCALLOPS)

Serves 6 people

500 g	linguini noodles
1 cup	sliced mushrooms
1 lb	scallops
2	shallots (chopped)
2	garlic cloves (crushed)
1/4 cup	white wine
4 cups	cream
1 tbsp	chopped parsley
1 cup	parmesan cheese
	salt and pepper to taste

Cook linguini in boiling salted water. Meanwhile saute scallops, shallots, mushrooms and garlic together for approx. 3 minutes, then add white wine, parsley and cream. Let reduce for an additional 5 minutes, strain linguini and add to the sauce. Add salt and pepper to taste and stir in parmesan cheese. Cook until sauce becomes thick and serve.

Comments:

Spaghetti Con Polpette

(SPAGHETTI AND MEATBALLS)

Serves 4 people

Preparation Time: 1 hour
Cooking Time: 1 1/2 hour

1/2 lb	ground veal
1/2 lb	ground pork
3	eggs
2 cups	grated parmesan cheese
500 grams	canned tomatoes
1	medium green pepper
2 cups	bread crumbs
3	garlic cloves, minced
1/2 cup	chopped parsley
500 grams	spaghetti
	salt and pepper to taste

Mix all ingredients in a large bowl. Make 1 inch round balls. In a skillet heat oil on high but not smoking, oil must be hot or the meatballs will stick, cook till brown on all sides for about 15 minutes. Remove some of the excess oil and add the onion, peppers, and parsley. Cook till soft; add the tomatoes and broth. Simmer on low heat for 1 hour. Cook spaghetti. Place cooked spaghetti in bowls and cover with sauce.

Comments:

Linguine Alle Vongole

(LINGUINI WITH CLAM SAUCE)

Serves 6 people

Preparation Time: 10 minutes
Cooking Time: 15 minutes

2 lbs	fresh baby clams, or 5 oz can
1/2 cup	olive oil
2	garlic cloves, minced
pinch	crushed chilies
pinch	oregano
5 sprigs	parsley, chopped fine
1 cup	dry white wine
1 lb	linguini

Wash and scrub fresh clams several times. In a large skillet, add oil and garlic. Cook over medium heat until garlic turns light brown. Add remaining ingredients and cover with a lid. When clams have opened, remove from the shell and return them to the skillet. Simmer for 5 minutes, stirring occasionally. Cook the pasta in an abundance of boiling, salted water. When pasta is partially cooked, drain and add to clam sauce. Mix well. Remove from heat and serve.

*when using canned clams, add clams and liquid to garlic along with the seasonings and wine.

Comments:

Spaghetti Carbonara

(SPAGHETTI WITH HAM AND EGGS)

Serves 4 – 6 people

Preparation Time: 5 minutes
Cooking Time: 15 minutes

2 tbsp	olive oil
8 oz	pancetta or bacon, diced
2	eggs
2	egg yolks
1 tbsp	cracked pepper
1/2 kg	spaghetti
	parmesan cheese to taste

Cook spaghetti in a generous amount of salted boiling water. Meanwhile in a saute pan heat olive oil and fry bacon. Strain oil. Add spaghetti. In a separate bowl mix eggs and pepper together. Add the mix to the spaghetti. Keep burner on medium heat and mix constantly while adding the cheese slowly. Add a small amount of water to make the sauce smooth.

Comments:

Pennette al Salmone

Serves 6 people

Preparation Time: 10 minutes
Cooking Time Sauce: 20 minutes
Cooking Time Pasta: 10 minutes

1 lb	penne
3 cups	whipping cream 32%
1/4 lb	chopped smoke salmone
2 cups	sliced fresh mushrooms
1/2 tsp	salt & pepper
1 tbsp	butter
1/2 cup	brandy
2	chopped shallots
3 tsp	parmigiano cheese

Put butter in a frying pan. Combine shallots, mushrooms and salmon and fry for 5 minutes. After frying for 5 minutes add 3 cups of whipping cream and cook for 20 minutes. Add salt, pepper and brandy. Cook pasta: cook penne in a generous amount of salted boiling water for 10 minutes. Drain water and put penne into the cooked sauce. Mix and sprinkle cheese on top. Ready to serve.

Comments:

Pasta Fresca con Uova

To make about ¾ pound

1 1/2 cups unsifted all-purpose flour

1 egg

1 egg white

1 tbsp olive oil

1 tsp salt

few drops water

Pour the flour into a large mixing bowl or in a heap on a pastry board, make a well in the center of the flour and in it put the egg, egg white, oil and salt. Mix together with a fork or your fingers until the dough can be gathered into a rough ball. Moisten any remaining dry bits of flour with drops of water and press them into the ball.

To make pasta by hand: knead the dough on a floured board, working in a little extra flour if the dough seems sticky. After about 10 minutes, the dough should be smooth, shiny and elastic. Wrap it in wax paper and let the dough rest for at least 10 minutes before rolling it.

Divide the dough into 2 balls. Place 1 ball on a floured board or pastry cloth and flatten it with the palm of your hand into an oblong about 1 inch thick. Dust the top lightly with flour. Then, using a heavy rolling pin, start at one end of the oblong and roll it out lengthwise away from yourself to within an inch or so of the farthest edge. Turn the dough crosswise and roll across its width. Repeat, turning and rolling the dough, until it is paper thin. If at any time the dough begins to stick, lift it carefully and sprinkle more flour under it.

To make cannelloni, tortellini and ravioli, follow the cutting directions in those recipes.

A pasta machine will do both the kneading and rolling. Pull off about a third of the dough at a time, set the smooth rolls of the pasta machine as far apart as possible and feed the piece of dough through them. Reroll this strip 4 or 5 more times, folding under the ragged edges and dusting the dough lightly with flour if it feels sticky. When the dough is smooth, shiny and elastic, it has been kneaded enough. Now start to roll it out, setting the machine to the second notch and feeding the dough through with the rolls closer together. Then set the machine at the third notch and roll the dough thinner. Repeat, changing the notch after each rolling, until the dough is about 1/16 inch thick.

Comments:

Ravioli

Pasta Dough

1 1/2 cups ricotta

3/4 cup   freshly grated imported
          parmesan cheese

2 tsp   grated onion

3   egg yolks

1 1/2 tsp salt

In a large mixing bowl, combine the 1 1/2 cups of ricotta, the 3/4 cup of grated Parmesan cheese, grated onion, 3 egg yolks and 1 1/2 teaspoons of salt and carefully stir them together until they are well mixed. Set aside until you have rolled out the dough.

Divide the pasta dough into four pieces and roll out the first one quarter of the dough to make it as thin as possible. Cover the rolled pasta with a damp towel to prevent its drying out, and roll out the second quarter of dough to a similar size and shape. Using the first sheet of rolled-out pastas as a sort of checkerboard, place a mound of about 1 tablespoon of the cheese-and-egg-yolk mixture every 2 inches across and down the pasta. Dip a pastry brush or your index finger into a bowl of water and make vertical and horizontal lines in a checkerboard pattern on the sheet of pasta, between the mounds of cheese filling. Be sure to use enough water to wet the lines evenly (the water will act as a bond to hold the finished ravioli together). Carefully spread the second sheet of rolled-out pasta on top of the first one, pressing down firmly around the filling and along the wetted lines. With a ravioli cutter, a pastry wheel or a small, sharp knife, cut the pasta into squares along the wetted lines. Separate the mounds of ravioli and set them aside on wax paper. In the same fashion, roll out, fill and cut the 2 other portions of dough.

To cook, drop the ravioli into 6 to 8 quarts of rapidly boiling salted water and stir them gently with a wooden spoon, to keep them from sticking to one another or to the bottom of the pot. Boil the ravioli for about 8 minutes, or until they are tender, then drain them thoroughly in a large sieve or colander. Serve the ravioli with tomato sauce or add butter and freshly grated Parmesan cheese, and gently stir them all together immediately before serving.

Comments:

Meat Filling

3 tbsp	butter
4 tbsp	finely chopped onions
3/4 lb	finely ground raw veal
1 ten oz	package frozen chopped spinach (defrosted, thoroughly squeezed and chopped again)
	or
3/4 lb	fresh spinach, cooked, squeezed and chopped
1/2 cup	freshly grated parmesan cheese
pinch	ground nutmeg
3	eggs
	salt

Melt the 3 tablespoons of butter in a small skillet and cook the onions, stirring frequently for about 7 or 8 minutes, or until they are soft and transparent but not brown. Add the 3/4 pound finely ground raw veal and cook, stirring constantly, until the veal loses its red colour and any accumulating liquid in the pan cooks completely away. Transfer the entire contents of the skillet to a mixing bowl and stir in the chopped spinach, grated Parmesan cheese and a pinch of nutmeg. In a separate bowl, beat the eggs lightly and add them to the onion, veal and spinach mixture. Taste and season with salt.

Comments:

Tortellini

(PASTA RINGS STUFFED WITH CHICKEN AND CHEESE)

To make about 80 (Serving 8 to 10)

Filling

2 1/4 cups	finely chopped cooked chicken (3 single chicken breasts boned and skinned, and poached in stock for 15 minutes)
1/2 cup	freshly grated imported parmesan cheese
2	egg yolks, lightly beaten
1/8 tsp	grated lemon peel
1/8 tsp	ground nutmeg
	salt
	freshly ground black pepper
1	double recipe of pasta dough
6–8 qts	water
	salt

Mix the chicken, cheese, egg yolks, lemon peel and nutmeg in a large bowl until they are thoroughly combined. Season with salt and pepper. Break off 1/4 of the pasta dough, and keep the rest moist by covering with foil or a damp cloth. Roll out the dough on a floured board until it is paper thin, then cut into 2 inch rounds with a biscuit cutter or a small glass. Place 1/4 teaspoon of the chicken mixture in the center of each round. Moisten the edges of each round. Fold the circles in half and press the edges firmly together. Shape into little rings by stretching the tips of each half circle slightly and wrapping the ring around your index finger. Gently press the tips together. The tortellini are best if they are cooked at once, but they may be covered with plastic wrap and refrigerated for a day or so.

Bring the water and salt to a boil in a heavy pot or kettle. Drop in the tortellini and stir gently with a wooden spoon for a moment to make sure they do not stick to one another. Boil, stirring occasionally, for about 8 minutes, or until they are tender. Drain them into a large sieve or colander. Serve with ragu bolognese or in hot beef or chicken stock.

Comments:

Main Courses

In The Fine Art of Italian Cooking, I included many of Molise's most well-known poultry, game and meat dishes. Here I have chosen a sampling of different recipes that are well known in the towns and provinces where they originated, and have not yet become popular elsewhere. I have tried to choose specialties from as many of the provinces as possible. The recipes feature only Molise's distinguished chicken, lamb, beef, pork and veal dishes.

Frutti di Mare

(FISH AND SEAFOOD)

There are many rivers in Molise and a coastline borders its entire length, so both freshwater and ocean fish are plentiful. The fish is so good, in fact, that most of the time it is cooked very simply: grilled over a wood fire or on a spit; deep-fried with the lightest of coatings, or poached and served with an uncooked herb sauce. But, of course, there are also dishes that are more complex and I present some of those here.

Although it is difficult to match some varieties of fish, sweet shrimp or tiny clams that come from the Adriatico, substitutions can be made and satisfying results can be achieved.

Funghi E Cape Sante Al Forno

(BAKED MUSHROOMS AND SCALLOPS)

Serves 2 people

Preparation Time: 5 minutes
Cooking Time: 20 minutes

12	large mushroom caps
12	scallops
1 cup	tomato sauce
1 cup	grated mozzarella cheese
	salt and pepper to taste

In escargot dishes, place mushroom caps in the holes of the dishes. Place one scallop on top of mushrooms. Season with salt and pepper. Pour over tomato sauce and cover with cheese. Bake for 20 minutes at 400 F.

Comments:

Antipasto Frutti Di Mare

(SEAFOOD ANTIPASTO)

Serves 6 people

Preparation Time: 15 minutes
Cooking Time: 30 minutes

Part A: Seafood

1 lb	squid, cleaned* and sliced crosswise 3/4 inch thick
1 lb	raw shrimp in shell
1 lb	scallops, sliced 1/2 inch thick
1	lemon, squeezed for juice

Slice scallops, wash shrimps (leaving them in the shell), clean squid and slice. Bring a large saucepan of salted water to a boil. Add seafood and lemon juice. Drop the lemon in the water and boil till cooked. Remove from heat and let seafood cool in water. Once cooled drain the seafood and peel the shrimp.

Part B: Dressing

2	garlic cloves, minced
2 tbsp	fresh parsley, chopped fine
1 cup	olive oil
1	lemon, squeezed for juice
dash	Worcestershire sauce
dash	tabasco sauce
	salt and pepper to taste

Combine garlic, parsley, oil, lemon juice, worcestershire sauce, tabasco sauce, salt and pepper. Mix well. Combine the seafood with the dressing. Marinate for 20 minutes or more. Serve on a bed of lettuce.

Comments:

Vongole Al Forno

(BAKED CLAMS)

Serves 6 people

Preparation Time: 10 minutes
Cooking Time: 25 minutes

2 lbs	fresh clams
1	chopped onion
2 tbsp	chopped parsley
1/2 cup	chopped, lightly smoked bacon
2 tbsp	olive oil
2 cups	tomato sauce
1/2 cup	parmesan cheese
1	garlic clove crushed

Saute onions, garlic and bacon together, add clams and parsley. Pour into baking dish and add tomato sauce. Sprinkle parmesan cheese on top. Bake at 350 F for 15 minutes.

Comments:

Cozze E Vongole Livornese

(MUSSELS AND CLAMS LIVORNO STYLE)

Serves 4 people

Preparation Time: 5 minutes
Cooking Time: 20 minutes

1 lb	mussels
1 lb	clams
1/2	onion diced
1 med	carrot diced
1	garlic clove, crushed
1/4 cup	olive oil
1 cup	white wine
	pinch chili peppers
	salt and pepper to taste

Heat oil and saute garlic, onions and carrots. Add mussels and clams with salt and pepper. Add chili peppers, wine and cover for about 10 minutes and serve.

Comments:

Calamari Ripieni

(STUFFED SQUID)

Serves 4 people

Preparation Time: 1 hour
Cooking Time: 30 minutes

1 1/2 lbs	whole calamari
1	garlic clove, crushed
2 tbsp	chopped parsley
3 tbsp	bread crumbs
1/2 cup	white wine
1 tbsp	olive oil
1	egg yolk
	salt and pepper to taste

Clean and peel squid, pull tentacles off. Chop together garlic, parsley, and tentacles. Mix this together with wine, olive oil, egg yolk and bread crumbs. Season with salt and pepper. Stuff each tube with the mixture and close each end with a toothpick. Place in a baking dish, rub with oil and season. Bake at 350 F for approx. 20–30 minutes.

Comments:

Gamberi Alla Provinciale

(SHRIMP WITH LEMON AND GARLIC)

Serves 1 person

Preparation Time: 15 minutes
Cooking Time: 5 minutes

2 tbsp	olive oil
8	large shrimp, shelled and deveined
1 tsp	parsley
2	garlic cloves, minced
1/4 cup	white wine
2 tbsp	butter
1/2	lemon, squeezed for the juice
	salt and pepper to taste

Combine a little flour with some salt and pepper and lightly roll shrimp in the flour. Shake to remove excess flour. Heat oil over high heat and saute shrimp about 1 minute per side, until just pink but not brown. Remove pan from heat and drain excess oil. Add remaining ingredients to pan and return to medium high heat, allowing sauce to boil. Swirl pan occasionally to combine ingredients. Bring to a simmer and cook about 1 minute in total. Sprinkle with freshly ground pepper. Serve with rice or pasta if desired.

Comments:

Trotelle Al Bleu

(POACHED TROUT)

Serves 4 people

Preparation Time: 5 minutes
Cooking Time: 15 minutes

4	fresh trout
3 cups	white vinegar
16 cups	water
	salt to taste
1	lemon, squeezed for the juice
1/2 cup	butter

Clean trout thoroughly. In a large pot bring salted water to a boil and add the vinegar and trout. Reduce heat and simmer for 10 minutes. Drain. In a small saucepan, melt butter and the lemon juice and stir. Pour sauce over the trout.

Comments:

Cozze Alla Marinara

(MUSSELS WITH MARINARA SAUCE)

Serves 6 people

Preparation Time: 5 minutes
Cooking Time: 10 minutes

7 lbs	fresh mussels
1/2 cup	olive oil
2 tsp	fresh parsley, chopped fine
1	bay leaf
1 tsp	thyme
1 cup	white wine
1	anchovy fillet in oil, chopped fine
2	garlic cloves, minced
	salt and pepper to taste

Scrub the mussels thoroughly; remove beard from the sides of the mussels and rinse several times. In a large saucepan add the olive oil, 1 tsp parsley, bay leaf, thyme and mussels. Pour in the wine and stir well. Cover and let cook over high heat. As soon as the mussels begin to open remove the saucepan from heat. Discard the bay leaf and remove the mussels. Strain the liquid and pour the liquid back into the saucepan and return to the heat. Add remaining butter, parsley, anchovy, garlic, salt and pepper. Stir well. Reduce heat and let simmer until sauce has thickened. Place mussels on a serving platter. Pour sauce over top and serve immediately.

Comments:

Gamberi Al Vino Bianco

(SHRIMP WITH WHITE WINE)

Serves 6 people

Preparation Time: 30 minutes
Cooking Time: 20 minutes

3 1/2 lbs	large shrimps, peeled and deveined
1/4 cup	oil
1 tbsp	butter
1	medium onion, diced fine
2	sticks of celery, chopped fine
1	medium carrot, chopped fine
1 1/2 cups	dry white wine
1/2 tsp	oregano
1/2 tsp	thyme
	salt and pepper to taste

In a large skillet saute onion, celery, and carrot in butter and oil over medium heat for about 5 minutes. Add shrimps and stir well. Cook for another 5 minutes. Add oregano, thyme, salt and pepper and stir well. Pour wine over shrimps and continue cooking on medium heat for about 15 minutes, stir occasionally.

Comments:

Salmone Al Funghi

(SALMON WITH MUSHROOMS)

Serves 4 people

Preparation Time: 5 minutes
Cooking Time: 15 minutes

4	6 oz. fresh salmon steaks
1/2 cup	butter
1 cup	fresh mushrooms, sliced thick
1	lemon, squeezed for the juice
	salt and pepper to taste

Flour and season with salt and pepper. Fry the salmon in butter and add the mushrooms. Place it in the oven for about 5 – 10 minutes or until you can pull the centre bone out. Remove from oven and sprinkle lemon juice over the top of the salmon.

Comments:

Spiedini Di Scampi

(SKEWERED SCAMPI)

Serves 4 – 6 people

Preparation Time: 20 minutes
Cooking Time: 10 minutes

2 1/2 lb	scampi, peeled and cleaned
3	thick slices of prosciutto, cubed
1/4 cup	softened butter
	lemon wedges
	salt and pepper to taste

Cut scampi in half then thread the scampi onto metal skewers alternating with cubed prosciutto. Sprinkle with salt and brush with butter. Place these in a non-stick roasting pan. Preheat oven to 400 F. Place roasting pan in oven and cook for 15 minutes. Baste with pan juices. When it is done remove from skewers and serve garnished with lemon wedges.

Comments:

Gamberetti Alla Portofino

(SHRIMP WITH TOMATO MUSHROOM SAUCE)

Serves 6 people

Preparation Time: 30 minutes
Cooking Time: 10 minutes

3 lbs	shrimp, peeled and deveined
1 cup	olive oil
3	garlic cloves, minced
2 cups	sliced mushrooms
1/2 cup	green peas
1 cup	white wine
2 cups	tomato sauce
1 cup	demi-glace
	salt and pepper to taste
1 tbsp	chopped parsley
500 grams	angel hair pasta

Heat oil in a saucepan, flour shrimp and saute for approximately 2 minutes. Add mushrooms, garlic, peas, wine, tomato sauce, and demi-glace. Season and continue cooking for a few minutes. Add parsley and stir. Pour the sauce over top of cooked angel hair pasta.

Comments:

Aragosta Di Pesaro

(LOBSTER IN LEMON SAUCE)

Serves 4 people

Preparation Time: 10 minutes
Cooking Time: 10 – 20 minutes

4	lobster tails
1	lemon
2	garlic cloves, minced
1/2 cup	white wine
1/2 cup	butter
1 tsp	chopped parsley
	salt and pepper to taste

Cut lobster tails lengthwise down the back and peel the meat out and rest it on the shell. Place on a baking sheet and in the oven at a temperatue of 350 F for 10 – 20 minutes. In a small saucepan heat wine, butter, lemon, garlic, parsley, and salt and pepper. Bring to a boil. The sauce should become thick, if it doesn't, add a little beurre manier.* Place lobster on a platter and pour sauce over top.

*Refer to page 19

Comments:

Aragosta Al Brandy

(LOBSTER WITH BRANDY SAUCE)

Serves 4 people

Preparation Time: 10 minutes
Cooking Time: 30 minutes

4	lobsters, (about 1 lb each)
1/2 cup	butter
1	garlic clove, minced
1/2 cup	brandy
1 tsp	fresh parsley, chopped fine
1 litre	32 % whipping cream
	salt and pepper to taste

Wash the lobster several times. Cut off the claws and crack the shells. Split each lobster in half lengthwise. Remove the sac of each lobster. Season lobster and claws with salt and pepper. In a large skillet melt butter and add the lobster, cook for 10 minutes on medium heat. Add the garlic, brandy, cream and cook for an additional 5 minutes. Remove the lobsters and claws and keep warm. Continue cooking sauce for about 15 minutes. Season sauce with more salt and pepper and add the parsley. Stir well. When ready to serve pour sauce over the lobsters and the claws. Serve with rice or pasta. Serve immediately.

Comments:

Scampi Alla Cardinale

(PRAWN CARDINAL STYLE)

Serves 4 people

Preparation Time: 10 minutes
Cooking Time: 15 minutes

2 lbs	scampi
1/4 lb	butter
1/4 cup	brandy
1/2 litre	32% whipping cream
2 cups	cooked tomato sauce
500 grams	linguini
	salt and pepper to taste

Cut scampi in half lengthwise and devein. Place in a baking dish and season with salt and pepper; cover with butter. Place in oven at 350 F for 5 minutes. Meanwhile cook linguini. When it is done, take the scampi out and place on a burner on medium heat. Add brandy, cream, and tomato sauce. Reduce heat until sauce thickens. Pour over cooked linguini.

Comments:

Pollo Alla Cacciatora

(CHICKEN ALLA HUNTER)

Serves 6 people

Preparation Time: 20 minutes
Cooking Time: 30 – 45 minutes

2 cups	chicken broth
1	4 lb chicken
1 cup	dry white wine
1/2 cup	olive oil
1/2 cup	flour
2	garlic cloves, minced
1 tsp	dried rosemary
6 sprigs	fresh parsley
2	anchovy fillets in oil
	salt and pepper to taste

Finely chop anchovy, garlic, parsley, rosemary, and mix well together. Set aside. Cut up chicken and season with salt and pepper. Flour all sides and shake off excess flour. In a large skillet heat oil and add chicken pieces and brown on all sides over medium heat. Remove skillet from the heat and discard excess oil, leaving the chicken pieces in the skillet. Return to heat and add chopped ingredients. Stir well. Pour wine over the chicken and continue cooking on low heat. Add chicken broth and bring to a boil and add beurre manier.* Continue cooking for 1/2 hour.

*Refer to page 19

Comments:

Petti Di Pollo Al Vino Bianco

(CHICKEN IN WHITE WINE)

Serves 6 people

Preparation Time: 10 minutes
Cooking Time: 20 minutes

6	boneless chicken breasts
1 cup	white wine
2 cups	chicken broth
1 tsp	rosemary
4	garlic cloves, minced
1 tbsp	parsley
1/2 cup	beurre manier
1/2 cup	olive oil

Heat oil in pan. Flour chicken and fry until done. Remove oil, add garlic and rosemary. Deglaze the pan with wine and broth. Add the parsley. Bring to a boil and add beurre manier* until sauce thickens slightly.

*Refer to page 19

Comments:

Pollo Alla Romana

(CHICKEN ROME STYLE)

Serves 4 people

Preparation Time: 20 minutes
Cooking Time: 1 hour

1	4 lb frying chicken
1 cup	sliced mushrooms
1	red pepper, sliced
1	green pepper, sliced
1	medium onion, sliced
3	garlic cloves, minced
1 tbsp	rosemary
1 tsp	chopped parsley
1 litre	chopped canned tomatoes
1 cup	olive oil
	salt and pepper to taste

Cut chicken into 8 pieces. Heat oil in pan. Flour and fry the chicken until brown. Put chicken in a large pot with the mushrooms, onions, peppers, garlic and rosemary. Add tomatoes and simmer for 1 hour. Add salt and pepper, and parsley. Serve over pasta.

Comments:

Pollastrella Alla Diavala

(CORNISH HEN WITH LEMON)

Serves 4 people

Preparation Time: 5 minutes
Cooking Time: 20 – 40 minutes

2	cornish hens, cut in half lengthwise
1/4 cup	oil
1 tbsp	butter
2	lemons, squeezed for the juice
	salt and pepper to taste

Season cornish hens with salt and pepper. Heat oil in saucepan until it smokes. Lay hens skin side down, and place in the oven at 400 F for 20 – 40 minutes or until it is done. Remove the hens from oven. Drain excess grease from the pan. Add butter and lemon juice.

Comments:

Pollo In Umido

(STEWED CHICKEN LEGS)

Serves 4 people

Preparation Time: 20 minutes
Cooking Time: 1 1/2 – 2 hours

8	chicken legs
4	medium potatoes, slice 1/2 inch thick
1	green pepper, sliced
1	red pepper, sliced
4	garlic cloves, minced
1 tsp	oregano
1 tbsp	chopped parsley
2 litres	canned tomatoes, chopped
1/2 litre	broth or water
	salt and pepper to taste

Mix all ingredients in a covered casserole dish and bake at 400 F for 1 1/2 hours.

Comments:

Petti Di Pollo Alla Milanese
(BREADED CHICKEN)

Serves 4 people

Preparation Time: 15 minutes
Cooking Time: 10 minutes

4	boneless chicken breasts
1/2 cup	flour
2 cups	bread crumbs
2	eggs
1/2 cup	milk
1/2 cup	olive oil

Pound chicken breasts until they are 2 – 3 times larger than original size. Dip the chicken in the flour and the egg mixture. Dip it into the breadcrumbs. Heat oil in frying pan and fry chicken until golden brown and remove.

Note:

2 eggs and 1/2 cup of milk mix together with fork.

Comments:

Arrosto Di Quaglie

(ROASTED QUAILS)

Serves 4 people

Preparation Time: 10 minutes
Cooking Time: 45 minutes

8	quails
4	shallots (diced)
4	slices of bacon (diced)
1/2 cup	white wine
2 cups	tomato sauce
	salt and pepper to taste

Season quails with salt and pepper and place in a baking dish, bake at 400 F for 20 minutes. Remove quails from the pan and place on a high burner, adding bacon and shallots. Cook for 5 minutes. Remove grease and add wine and tomato sauce. Place quails back into pan and let cook for another 5 minutes and serve.

Comments:

Wild Duck Antonietta

Serves 2 – 4 people

1 medium duck

pinch   garlic salt

2–3 sprigs thyme, fresh or powdered

1 pt   vegetable oil

         salt and pepper to taste

Cut duck into 4 to 6 parts. Generously sprinkle garlic salt, thyme, salt and pepper over duck pieces, then dip into flour. Deep fry duck pieces in a 10 inch frying pan in vegetable oil. Fry 10–15 minutes, depending on how you like your duck done. If you use fresh thyme, add 2 or 3 sprigs after duck has been frying about 5 minutes and turn once.

The perfect accompaniment with duck prepared in this manner is a good green salad with olive oil and vinegar dressing.

Comments:

Pollo Alle Mandorle

(CHICKEN WITH ALMONDS)

Serves 6 people

Preparation Time: 10 minutes
Cooking Time: 20 minutes

6	boneless chicken breasts
1 1/2 cups	sliced almonds (toasted)
1 cup	marsala wine
2 cups	demi-glace
1 cup	water
	salt and pepper to taste

Heat oil in a large skillet and dredge chicken in flour and fry on each side for approximately 3 minutes. Drain oil, add almonds and marsala wine. Then add demi-glace and water. Reduce heat, let reduce, add salt and pepper to taste.

Comments:

Pollo Ai Funghi Freschi

(CHICKEN WITH FRESH MUSHROOMS)

Serves 4 people

Preparation Time: 20 minutes
Cooking Time: 30 – 45 minutes

1	3 lb chicken, cut in pieces
1/4 cup	olive oil
1 tbsp	parsley, chopped fine
1	garlic clove, minced
	salt to taste
2 cups	fresh mushrooms, sliced thick
3/4 lb	ripe tomatoes, peeled and diced
3 – 4 tbsp	chicken broth

In a large skillet heat oil on high heat. Add chicken pieces and brown on all sides. Add parsley, garlic, and salt. Stir well. Reduce heat and add mushrooms, and cook for 10 minutes. Then add tomatoes, chicken broth. Continue cooking for another 30 minutes or until chicken is done, stirring frequently.

Comments:

Pollo Ripieno

(STUFFED CORNISH HEN)

Serves 2 people

Preparation Time: 15 minutes
Cooking Time: 1 hour

1	cornish hen
1/2	green pepper, diced small
1 tbsp	garlic cloves, crushed
2	eggs
2	basil leaves, chopped
1 cup	bread crumbs
1 cup	parmesan cheese
	salt and pepper to taste
1	carrot, diced small
1	celery stalk, diced small
2 cups	white wine

Mix stuffing ingredients in a large bowl until firm, then stuff hen. Roast hen at 400 F for one half hour in a baking dish. Then add carrot, celery and wine to the bottom of the dish and continue cooking for another one half hour. Remove from the oven and split the hen in two. Pour sauce on top.

Comments:

Fagiani Con Porcini

(PHEASANT WITH PORCINI SAUCE)

Serves 2 people

Preparation Time: 10 minutes
Cooking Time: 20 minutes

2	boneless pheasant breasts
25 grams	dried porcini mushroom
1 cup	demi-glace
1/2 cup	barolo wine
1	shallot diced
1/2 cup	hot water
	salt and pepper to taste

Soak porcini in a 1/2 cup of hot water. Meanwhile heat skillet with oil and dredge pheasant in flour, brown each side for 2 minutes. Drain grease and place in 350 F oven for 10 minutes. Remove breasts, add shallot and mushrooms and place in skillet on heat with the wine and juice from the mushrooms. Add demi-glace, reduce heat until the mixture is thick. Season with salt and pepper and pour over breasts.

*Wild game should always be well cooked.

Comments:

Bistecca Alla Zingara

(BEEF GYPSY STYLE)

Serves 4 people

Preparation Time: 10 minutes
Cooking Time: 10 – 20 minutes

4	8 oz. New York steaks
1	red pepper, sliced
1	green pepper, sliced
1 cup	sliced mushrooms
1/2 cup	marsala wine
2 cups	demi-glace
1 tsp	chopped parsley
	salt and pepper to taste

Heat saute pan with a touch of olive oil. Cook steaks as desired. Remove steaks from pan, add peppers and mushrooms. Saute for 2 minutes. Deglaze pan with marsala wine, add demi-glace, salt and pepper. Bring to a boil and add parsley. Place on platter and pour over beef.

Comments:

Bistecca Alla Pizzaiola

(BEEF IN WINE AND TOMATO SAUCE)

Serves 4 people

Preparation Time: 15 minutes
Cooking Time: 10 – 20 minutes

8	4 oz beef tenderloin
3 tbsp	olive oil
2	garlic cloves, minced
1/2 cup	dry white wine
1	28 oz can tomatoes, chopped with liquid
	salt and pepper to taste

Heat oil in a large skillet. When oil is hot, saute beef tenderloin for about 2 minutes per side. Remove from skillet and set aside. In the same skillet, add garlic, wine, tomatoes, salt and pepper. Simmer for 15 minutes over low heat, stirring frequently. Return tenderloin to skillet and continue to simmer for another 10 minutes (or longer if you prefer the tenderloin well done). When ready to serve, place tenderloin on plates and pour sauce over the top.

Comments:

Filetto Di Manzo Al Vino Rosso

(BEEF IN RED WINE SAUCE)

Serves 6 people

Preparation Time: 15 minutes
Cooking Time: 10 – 20 minutes

12	4 oz beef tenderloin
4 tbsp	olive oil
1 lb	fresh mushrooms, sliced thick
4	shallots, sliced fine
1 1/2 cups	dry red wine
3 tbsp	butter
	salt and pepper to taste

Heat oil in a large skillet. When oil is hot, saute fillet for about 2 minutes per side. Remove fillets and keep warm. Add mushrooms and shallots, let cook for about 5 minutes. Season with salt and pepper. Pour wine into the skillet and let boil for about 5 minutes. Add butter and stir well. Return fillet to the skillet and continue cooking until sauce has reduced, approximately 5 to 10 minutes (or longer if you prefer the fillet well done). When ready to serve, place fillet on plates and pour sauce over top.

Comments:

Filetto Di Manzo In Agrodolce

(SWEET AND SOUR BEEF)

Serves 4 people

Preparation Time: 5 minutes
Cooking Time: 5 – 20 minutes

8	4 oz filet of beef
2 cups	sliced mushrooms
2 tbsp	butter
1/4 cup	balsamic vinegar
3 cups	demi-glace
1 cup	broth
	salt and pepper to taste

Season filet with salt and pepper. Melt butter in a frying pan and add beef and fry till desired colour. Remove beef from the pan, then add mushrooms and saute for 1 – 2 minutes. Add vinegar, demi-glace, and broth. Place filets on platter and pour sauce over top.

Comments:

Abbacchio Alla Toscana

(RACK OF LAMB)

Serves 4 people

Preparation Time: 10 minutes
Cooking Time: 20 – 30 minutes

4	racks of lamb
1 tsp	butter
4	shallots
1 tsp	rosemary
2	garlic cloves, minced
1 tsp	cracked pepper
1 cup	red wine
1 cup	demi-glace
	salt and pepper to taste

Sear lamb in a saucepan, then put lamb in a 350 F oven until desired colour. Meanwhile in a small pot melt butter and add the shallots, rosemary, garlic, and pepper. Saute for 2 – 3 minutes and add wine and demi-glace. Bring to a boil and reduce to a sauce consistency. Add salt and strain. Remove the lamb from oven and let rest for 5 – 10 minutes before cutting. Place lamb on platter and pour sauce over top.

Comments:

Agnello Alla Cacciatora

(LAMB ALLA HUNTER)

Serves 4 – 6 people

Preparation Time: 20 minutes
Cooking Time: 1/2 hour

2 cups	chicken broth
4 lbs	lamb
1 cup	white wine
1/2 cup	olive oil
1/2 cup	flour
6	parsley sprigs
1 tsp	dried rosemary
2	garlic cloves
2	anchovy fillets (in oil)
	salt and pepper to taste

Finely chop anchovy, garlic, rosemary, and parsley. Mix together well and set aside. Season lamb pieces with salt and pepper. Flour all sides and shake off excess. In a large skillet heat oil and add lamb pieces. Brown on all sides over medium heat. Remove skillet from heat and discard oil leaving lamb pieces in skillet. Return to heat and add chopped ingredients. Stir well. Pour wine over lamb and continue cooking on low heat. Add chicken broth, stir and reduce heat. Thicken with beurre manier* and continue cooking for 1/2 hour.

*Refer to page 19

Comments:

Cotolette D'Agnello Alla Milanese

(BREADED LAMB CHOPS)

Serves 6 people

Preparation Time: 20 minutes
Cooking Time: 10 minutes

6	lamb chops
1/2 cup	flour
1	egg, beaten
2 cups	bread crumbs
1 tbsp	butter
1/4 cup	olive oil
	salt and pepper to taste

Pound lamb chops firmly with a flat surfaced mallet until each chop is 2 – 3 times larger in size. Season with salt and pepper. Coat each chop with flour and shake off excess flour. Then dip into egg. Coat well with bread crumbs. In a large skillet heat oil and butter. Add the lamb chops and saute over medium heat until golden brown (about 10 – 15 minutes). Serve immediately with vegetables or pasta.

Comments:

Cosciotto D'Agnello Arrosto

(ROASTED LEG OF LAMB)

Serves 6 – 8 people

Preparation Time: 10 minutes
Cooking Time: 1 hour

1 (approx. 3 lbs)	leg of lamb
1 cup	oil
1 cup	white wine
2	garlic cloves, minced
1 tsp	rosemary
	salt and pepper
	to taste

With a knife cut slits about an inch long and 1/4 inch deep into the leg of lamb. Lightly press garlic and rosemary into slits and season with salt and pepper. Place leg of lamb into a roasting pan and pour oil over top. Place into a preheated oven 400 F and cook for about 1/2 hour. Baste occasionally with pan juices. Pour wine over the top and continue cooking for another 1/2 hour. Turn frequently and continue basting. When ready to serve place leg of lamb on a platter and pour juices over top.

Comments:

Fegato Di Vitella Con Cipolla

(CALF LIVER WITH ONIONS)

Serves 2 people

Preparation Time: 10 minutes
Cooking Time: 5 minutes

1 lb	calves liver, sliced thinly
1 med	onion sliced very thinly
2	lemons
1/2 cup	olive oil
	salt and pepper to taste

Heat olive oil and add onions to the pan. Start to brown them and add liver. Continue cooking on high for 2 minutes. Add salt and pepper and lemon juice. Then serve.

Comments:

Cotollette Alla Milanese

(BREADED VEAL CHOPS)

Serves 6 people

Preparation Time: 15 minutes
Cooking Time: 20 minutes

6	veal chops
1/2 cup	flour
1	egg, beaten
1/2 cup	bread crumbs
1/2 cup	oil
1 tbsp	butter
	salt and pepper to taste

Pound veal chops firmly with a flat surfaced mallet until each chop is 2 – 3 times larger in size. Season with salt and pepper. Coat both sides with flour and shake off excess. Then dip into beaten egg. Coat well with bread crumbs. In a large skillet heat oil and butter and add veal chops and saute them over medium heat until golden brown approximately 10 – 15 minutes. Serve with vegetables or pasta.

Comments:

Involtini Di Vitello

(STUFFED VEAL)

Serves 4 people

Preparation Time: 30 minutes
Cooking Time: 15 minutes

12 2 oz	veal scaloppini
12	slices of capicollo (stuffing)
1/2 lb	mozzarella cheese, diced small
1/2 lb	cooked mushrooms, chopped fine
1 tbsp	chopped parsley
2	egg yolks
1/4 cup	marsala wine
1/4 cup	grated parmesan cheese (sauce)
1/4 cup	white wine
1/4 cup	demi-glace
1/8 cup	broth

Pound veal until they are 2 – 3 times larger. Place one piece of capicollo on each piece of veal. In a large bowl mix the stuffing ingredients together and mix thoroughly. Place a tsp. of the mixture on the centre of the veal and fold lengthwise. Place skillet on medium heat and add oil. Flour meat and brown on both sides and set veal aside. Remove oil from pan and add white wine. Add demi-glace, broth, salt and pepper and reduce sauce. Place veal on plate and pour sauce over the top.

Comments:

Polpettone

Polpettone

(VEAL MEAT LOAF)

Serves 4 – 6 people

Preparation Time: 20 minutes
Cooking Time: 1 hour

3	garlic cloves, minced
1 lb	ground veal
1 tbsp	fresh parsley, chopped fine
6	eggs
3 cups	grated parmesan cheese
	salt and pepper to taste
1 tbsp	oil
1/2 cup	capicollo, chopped
2 cups	dry white wine

In a large bowl mix garlic, ground veal, parsley, 4 eggs, cheese, salt and pepper. Mix well until blended. Set aside. Beat 2 eggs. In skillet pour oil into the centre and add the beaten eggs. Stir constantly until eggs are set. Remove from heat and set aside. With moistened hands shape meat mixture into a large square patty about 1/2 inch thick. Spread egg mixture and chopped capicollo and parsley over meat layer leaving a 1/4 inch edge. Roll starting from outer edge and form into a loaf. Preheat oven at 350 F and pour 1/4 inch oil in a baking pan and place in oven. Remove when oil is heated. Carefully place meatloaf in pan and cook for 50 minutes. Remove from oven and pour wine over top and return to oven for another 10 minutes. Slice and serve hot.

Comments:

Bracioline Alla Panna Con Funghi

(VEAL SCALOPPINI WITH MUSHROOMS AND CREAM SAUCE)

Serves 6 people

Preparation Time: 30 minutes
Cooking Time: 15 minutes

2 lbs	white veal, trim away fat and membrane
1/2 cup	flour
1/4 cup	oil
2 tbsp	butter
1 cup	fresh mushrooms, sliced thick
1/2 cup	dry white wine
1 1/2 cup	32% whipping cream
	salt and pepper to taste

Cut veal into 12 pieces. Pound each piece of veal using a flat surfaced mallet until each piece is 3 times larger in size. Season each veal scaloppini with salt and pepper. Flour both sides and shake off excess. In a large skillet heat oil and butter over medium heat. Add veal scaloppini and cook each side for about 2 minutes. Add mushrooms. Let cook for 5 minutes. Discard oil leaving veal scaloppini and mushrooms in the skillet. Add wine, cream, salt and pepper. Continue cooking for 4 to 10 minutes. Remove veal scaloppini and place it on a platter keeping warm. Continue to reduce sauce further on low heat. When ready to serve, pour sauce over top of the veal scaloppini. Serve with vegetables.

Comments:

Piccata Al Limone

(VEAL SCALOPPINI IN LEMON SAUCE)

Serves 4 – 6 people

Preparation Time: 30 minutes
Cooking Time: 15 minutes

12	veal scaloppine, pounded
1/2 cup	flour
1/2 cup	oil
3 tbsp	butter
1 cup	dry white wine
5 sprigs	parsley, chopped finely
2 cups	chicken broth
1	lemon, squeezed for juice
	salt and pepper to taste

Pound each piece of veal firmly with flat surfaced mallet until each piece is 2 – 3 times larger in size. Season with salt and pepper. Lightly flour and shake off excess. In a large heavy skillet heat oil and 1 tbsp. butter over high heat and add veal scaloppine. Cook each side for 2 minutes. Discard oil and leave veal in skillet. Add wine, parsley, broth, and lemon juice on veal. Stir until blended. Lower heat and reduce sauce further using beurre manier.* Simmer for about 5 minutes. Remove from heat. Place veal on plates and pour sauce over top. Serve with vegetables.

*Refer to page 19

Comments:

Nodini Al Pomodoro & Funghi

(VEAL CHOPS WITH TOMATO AND MUSHROOMS)

Serves 6 people

Preparation Time: 20 minutes
Cooking Time: 30 minutes

6	veal chops
1/4 cup	olive oil
1 tbsp	butter
1	small onion, diced fine
2 cups	fresh mushrooms, sliced thick
1/2 cup	white wine
1	garlic clove, minced
2	sage leaves, fresh or dried
1 cup	ripe tomatoes, peeled and diced
1 cup	chicken broth
	salt and pepper to taste

Season veal chops on both sides with salt and pepper. In a large skillet heat oil and butter, add veal chops and brown quickly on both sides turning frequently. Saute for about 5 minutes. Remove veal chops from skillet and add onions and mushrooms. Cook until onions become soft and then return veal to skillet and stir well. Add garlic, sage, wine and tomatoes. Stir and cook over medium heat for 20 minutes and if the sauce is reducing add the chicken broth. Place veal chops on a platter and pour sauce over top. Serve with vegetables or pasta.

Comments:

144

Sella Di Vitello

(ROAST SADDLE OF VEAL)

Serves 6 people

Preparation Time: 10 minutes
Cooking Time: 45 – 90 minutes

5 – 6 lbs	veal roast (saddle)
1 cup	mushrooms, sliced thick
1/2 cup	medium diced onion
1 cup	chicken broth
1 cup	white wine
	salt and pepper to taste

Place veal roast in a baking dish and season well with salt and pepper. Place in a 400 F oven. Cook until medium or well done. Add mushrooms, onions to the bottom of the pan continue cooking for at least 5 minutes. Then add broth and wine let reduce by half. Remove roast from pan and slice, then pour sauce over top and serve.

Comments:

Sella Di Vitello

Saltimbocca Alla Romana

(VEAL WITH HAM)

Serves 6 people

Preparation Time: 20 minutes
Cooking Time: 10 minutes

2 lbs	veal, trimmed and membrane removed
12 slices	capicolla or prosciutto
12 pcs	fresh sage
1/4 cup	white wine
1/2 cup	demi-glace
1/2 cup	chicken broth

Cut veal into 12 pieces, pound each piece of veal using a flat surface mallet, until each piece is 3 times larger in size, season each piece with salt and pepper. Place one piece of sage and capicolla on top of the veal and pound together. Heat oil in skillet and flour each side of the veal, fry for approx. 2–3 minutes. Continue cooking for another 2 minutes and add wine, demi-glace and broth. Remove veal and place on plates, let sauce reduce until desired thickness and pour over top of veal.

Comments:

Vitello Alla Parmigiana

(VEAL PARMIGIANA)

Serves 6 people

Preparation Time: 20 minutes
Cooking Time: 10 minutes

6	1/4 lb. pieces of veal scaloppini
12	thin slices mozzarella cheese
24 oz	cooked tomato sauce
	bread crumbs
	flour
	egg and milk mix

Pound veal until pieces are 2 – 3 times larger than original size. Dredge in flour, then repeat in the egg and milk mixture. After bread the veal with breadcrumbs. In a saucepan heat a fair amount of oil on high. Fry veal until golden brown, remove from pan and place on a baking sheet. Pour tomato sauce on top of the veal and lay slice of mozzarella on top. Place in a 400 F oven until cheese is melted.

Comments:

Osso Buco

Serves 6 people

Preparation Time: 15 minutes
Cooking Time: 1 1/2 hours

6	veal shank (2 inch thick)
1	carrot, diced
1	onion, diced
1	celery stalk, diced
2 litres	tomato sauce
2 litres	demiglace
	salt and pepper

Season shank with salt and pepper. Dredge in flour. In a saucepan heat a fair amount of oil on high. Fry shank on both sides until brown. Remove from pan and place in a baking pan. In the same frying pan with a little oil sauté carrots, onion, celery and pat on top of shank. Add tomato sauce and demiglace. Bake in oven at 375 F for 1 1/2 hours or until meat is tender.

Comments:

151

Zucchini Al Pomodoro

(ZUCCHINI WITH TOMATO)

Serves 2 people

Preparation Time: 5 minutes
Cooking Time: 5 minutes

1 tbsp	butter
1	small zucchini
1/2 cup	tomato sauce
1	garlic clove, crushed
1/4 cup	white wine
	salt and pepper to taste

Slice zucchini into 1/2 inch slices. Place butter in a pan on medium heat and saute zucchini for 2 minutes. Add garlic and wine, let cook for another 30 seconds. Add tomato sauce, salt and pepper. Cook for another 2 minutes and serve.

Comments:

Cavolfiore Alla Milanese

(FRIED CAULIFLOWER)

Serves 6 people

Preparation Time: 20 minutes
Cooking Time: 30 minutes

1	large cauliflower
2	eggs, beaten
1/4 cup	oil
3 tbsp	butter
	bread crumbs
	salt to taste

Remove outer leaves from cauliflower. Bring water to a boil in a large saucepan and add the cauliflower whole. Cook for about 15 minutes. Drain. Cool and break into florets. Dip cauliflower into flour and then into the egg. Coat with breadcrumbs. In a large skillet, heat oil and butter until very hot. Add cauliflower, reduce heat and fry for 10 minutes or until golden brown.

Comments:

Carciofi Fritti

(FRIED ARTICHOKES)

Serves 4 people

Preparation Time: 20 minutes
Cooking Time: 10 minutes

6	tender artichokes
1	lemon, squeeze for the juice
1	egg, beaten
	flour
	oil for frying
	salt to taste

Put the lemon juice into a bowl of cold water. Wash artichokes and trim off the outer leaves and the stems. Slice vertically into quarters and immediately drop them into the water/lemon mixture. In a medium saucepan heat oil until very hot. Dip artichokes into the beaten egg. Roll artichokes into flour to coat. Shake off excess. Fry until crispy and golden brown. Sprinkle with salt and serve.

Comments:

Asparagi Alla Besciamella

(ASPARAGUS IN WHITE SAUCE)

Serves 6 people

3 lbs	fresh asparagus
1/4 cup	soft butter
1/4 lb	prosciutto, sliced thin
2 cups	bechamel sauce
1/2 cup	grated parmesan cheese

Preheat oven to 350 F. Wash asparagus and scrape stems with a knife. Arrange the asparagus in a bunch with the tips even. Tie together at the bottom with thread and even off the ends by slicing with a sharp knife. Stand the asparagus tips up in a tall pot. Add enough cold water to cover the stems. Bring to a boil, then reduce heat and simmer for 10 minutes. Remove from heat and transfer asparagus to a chopping board. Untie and cut off the hard white ends. Place asparagus in a bowl and add butter, mixing well. Wrap a slice of prosciutto around 3 or 4 spears and place in buttered baking dish. Cover with bechamel sauce and sprinkle with grated parmesan cheese. Bake in the oven for about 15 – 20 minutes or until golden brown in colour.

Comments:

Asparagi In Salsa Maionese

(ASPARAGUS WITH MAYONNAISE)

Serves 6 people   *Preparation Time: 15 minutes*

30	cooked Asparagus (fresh or frozen)
2 cups	olive oil
6	egg yolks
1	piece of lemon
	tabasco to taste
	worcestershire sauce
	salt & pepper to taste

Place egg yolks in a large mixing bowl and slowly whisk in oil until completely absorbed, then add lemon juice, tabasco, worcestershire, salt and pepper. Place asparagus on plates and pour a little sauce over the asparagus.

Comments:

Broccoli Romani Al'Aglio

(FRIED BROCCOLI)

Serves 4 people

Preparation Time: 5 minutes
Cooking Time: 10 minutes

1	bunch broccoli
3 tbsp	olive oil
2	garlic cloves, minced
1/2 cup	dry white wine
	salt and pepper to taste

Wash broccoli and cut into florets. Add broccoli to a large saucepan of boiling, salt water and cook till bright green and stems are soft. Heat oil medium saucepan. Add garlic and saute until light brown. Add broccoli and sprinkle with pepper. Saute for 2 minutes. Then pour wine overtop and continue cooking for another 2 minutes.

Comments:

Cavoletti Di Bruxelle, Con Pancetta, Alla Vastese

(BRUSSEL SPROUTS WITH BACON)

Serves 4 people

Preparation Time: 5 minutes
Cooking Time: 15 minutes

1 lb	fresh brussel sprouts
1/4 lb	bacon, chopped
1 tbsp	butter
	salt and pepper to taste

Place washed brussel sprouts in a saucepan with a small amount of boiling salted water. Cook for about 15 minutes, or until tender. Drain. In a medium saucepan, melt butter on high heat. Add bacon and fry for about 10 minutes. Add brussel sprouts and pepper, mixing well. Continue cooking for about 5 minutes before serving.

Comments:

Pepperoni Alla Romana

(PEPPERS STUFFED WITH PASTA)

Serves 4 people

Preparation Time: 30 minutes
Cooking Time: 30 minutes

4 large	sweet green peppers
2 cups	baby pasta shells cooked
16 cups	water
3 cups	spaghetti sauce
2 tbs.	salt
1/4 cup	parmesan cheese
1/3 cup	chopped chives or green onions
1/2 tsp	oregano
dash	hot pepper flakes (optional)
3/4 cup	grated mozzarella cheese
	salt and pepper to taste

Remove tops of peppers and reserve. core, seed and blanch peppers and tops in boiling water for 5 minutes. In a large pot, bring water and salt to a boil. Add pasta and cook uncovered. Stir pasta occasionally until cooked, but still firm. Drain well. Combine the hot, cooked pasta with 1 1/2 cups of spaghetti sauce, parmesan cheese, chives and spices. Stuff each pepper with the pasta mixture. Top each with the grated mozzarella cheese and replace pepper lid. Stand peppers in a baking dish and pour remainder of sauce around the peppers. Cover dish with foil and bake in a 375 F oven for 30 minutes or until tender, but not limp. Serve immediately.

Comments:

Frittata Con Carciofi

(ARTICHOKE OMELETTE)

Serves 4 people

Preparation Time: 10 minutes
Cooking Time: 30 minutes

4	pork sausage sliced
1/2	onion chopped
1	garlic clove (crushed)
1	can of artichokes sliced
4	beaten eggs
1 tsp	chopped parsley
	salt and pepper
1/3 cup	parmesan cheese

Saute sausage, onions and garlic together. Then add artichokes with salt and pepper. Stir in eggs and pour into a buttered baking dish. Add cheese and parsley. Bake at 350 F for 20 minutes.

Comments:

L'Aglio Arosto

(ROASTED GARLIC SMASHED POTATOES)

Serves 4 people

2 lbs	baking potatoes, peeled and cut into large chunks
1 tbsp	unsalted butter
	Salt and pepper to taste
2 tbsp	chopped chives
1/2 cup	heavy cream
1/2 cup	Consorzio roasted garlic olive oil

Cook potatoes in large pot of boiling, salted water until fork tender. Drain and let dry on baking pan 5 minutes. In large bowl, begin mashing potatoes with butter using an electric mixer. Heat cream to a boil; add to potatoes and continue to beat. Add Consorzio roasted garlic olive oil and beat again. Season with salt and pepper to taste. Beat in chives. If too thick, thin with warm milk. Reheat if necessary (this is most easily done in a microwave oven).

Comments:

Patate Al Lesso

(BOILED POTATOES)

Serves 6 people

Preparation Time: 5 minutes
Cooking Time: 30 – 50 minutes

2 lbs	potatoes, sliced thin
2 tbsp	fresh parsley, chopped fine
	salt to taste

Peel potatoes and cut in medium sized pieces. Bring salted water to boil in a large pot. Add potatoes and cook on low heat for about 35 minutes. Drain. Place potatoes in serving bowl and sprinkle with parsley. Mix well.

Comments:

Patate Al Forno Con Rosmarino

(BAKED POTATOES)

Serves 6 people

Preparation Time: 10 minutes
Cooking Time: 30 – 50 minutes

2 lbs	potatoes, sliced thin
1/2 cup	oil
4 tbsp	butter
2 tsp	dried rosemary
	salt to taste

Preheat oven to 350 F. Peel potatoes and cut in thin slices. In a large skillet, heat oil and butter until very hot. Add potatoes and sprinkle with salt and rosemary. Saute for about 5 minutes, stirring constantly. Place skillet in the oven to continue cooking for another 30 minutes, stirring occasionally.

Comments:

Patate Alla Paesana

(FRIED POTATOES WITH ONION)

Serves 6 people

Preparation Time: 10 minutes
Cooking Time: 30 – 50 minutes

2 lbs	potatoes, sliced thin
3	onions, sliced thick
1/4 cup	olive oil
2 tbsp	butter
	salt and pepper to taste

Peel potatoes and cut into thin slices. In a large skillet, heat olive oil and butter. Add onions and saute until soft. Add potatoes and season with salt and pepper. Fry for abut 30 minutes on medium heat, stirring frequently.

Comments:

Risotto Con Funghi

(RICE WITH MUSHROOMS)

Serves 6 people

Preparation Time: 10 minutes
Cooking Time: 1/2 hour

4 cups	uncooked rice (Italian short grained)
2 cups	fresh mushrooms, finely sliced
1	onion, diced
8 – 10 cups	chicken broth
1/4 cup	grated parmesan cheese
1/3 cup	butter

Saute onion in butter over medium heat in a sauce pot. When the onion becomes soft, add the mushrooms and stir. Heat the chicken broth and add the rice. Reduce the heat and cook for 1/2 hour or until rice is tender. Stir frequently. Remove from heat. Stir in the remaining butter and the grated parmesan cheese.

Comments:

Risotto Portofino

Serves 4 people

Preparation Time: 20 minutes
Cooking Time: 30 minutes

3 cup	risotto (Italian short grain rice)
1 cup	green peas
2	cloves of garlic (crushed)
1 1/2 cup	sliced mushrooms
2 tbsp	chopped parsley
1/4 cup	white wine
1 lb.	shrimp
6 cup	tomato sauce
1 cup	parmesan cheese
	salt and pepper to taste

Cook 3 cups of rice in 2 litres of salted boiling water for 20 minutes. Meanwhile, saute shrimps, mushrooms, and garlic together for approximately 1 minute. Add wine, parsley, green peas and tomato sauce. Simmer for an additional 2 minutes. Remove half the mixture from pan and set aside. Strain rice and add it to the sauce, stir in cheese. Place the rice on plates and add shrimp. Pour remaining sauce over top.

Comments:

Risotto Pescatora

(RICE ALLA FISHERMAN)

Serves 6 – 8 people

Preparation Time: 20 minutes
Cooking Time: 30 minutes

1 lb	baby clams
12	large shrimp, shelled and deveined
12	large squid, cleaned
1/2 cup	olive oil
1 tbsp	butter
1	medium onion, diced
1	garlic clove, minced
1/2 cup	dry white wine
1/2 lb	fresh mushrooms, sliced thin
4 cups	rice, uncooked
2 litre	chicken broth
	salt and pepper to taste

Wash and scrub clams. Slice the shrimp into bite size pieces. Cut the squid into 3/4 inch crosswise thick pieces. In a large saucepot saute onion, and garlic for 5 minutes and add seafood. Stir well. Cook for another 5 minutes. Add wine and simmer for 10 minutes. Add a little water and stir occasionally. Add mushrooms, salt and pepper. Stir well. Remove clams. Add rice and chicken broth. Continue cooking for 20 minutes, stirring occasionally. When ready to serve garnish with rice and clams.

Comments:

Risotto Zafferano
(RICE WITH SAFFRON)

Serves 2 people

Preparation Time: 5 minutes
Cooking Time: 30 minutes

1/2 cup	risotto
1 1/2 cups	chicken broth
pinch	saffron
1/4 cup	parmesan cheese
	salt and pepper to taste

Place rice in boiling chicken broth and cook for approximately 20 minutes, stirring continuously. Add salt, pepper, and a pinch of saffron. Then stir in parmesan cheese. Let cook until rice becomes sticky and serve.

Comments:

Crocante

(RICE CROQUETTE)

Serves 8 people

Preparation Time: 4 hours
Cooking Time: 10 minutes

4 cups	rice
3	eggs
2 cups	parmesan cheese
	chopped parsley
2 cups	bread crumbs
	salt and pepper to taste
2 cups	olive oil

Cook rice in 2 litres of water for 20 minutes. Strain and let cool in refrigerator for approximately 3 hours. Mix rice with eggs, cheese, bread crumbs, salt and pepper. Make sure the mix is fairly stiff, add more bread crumbs if necessary. Form mixture into 1 1/2 inch balls. Heat oil and fry balls until golden brown.

Comments:

Risotto Con Scampi

(RICE WITH SCAMPI SAUCE)

Serves 6 – 8 people

Preparation Time: 20 minutes
Cooking Time: 40 minutes

Part A: Rice

2 lbs	scampi, medium size
2 litres	water
1 tbsp	butter
1/4 cup	olive oil
5 cups	rice
1/2	medium onion

Split the scampi in half. Remove from shell. Set scampi aside. Place the shells in a large saucepot of boiling salted water. Let boil for 20 minutes. Meanwhile in a skillet saute onion in butter and oil for about 5 minutes over medium heat. Add rice and stir well. Strain the scampi broth and discard the shells. Add broth to rice and stir well with a wooden spoon. Let cook for 20 minutes.

Part B: Mix Sauce

5	medium shallots, diced
1	garlic clove, minced
2 tbsp	butter
1/2 cup	brandy
1 tbsp	parsley
5 cups	tomato sauce
2 cups	whipping cream

In a skillet saute shallots and garlic in butter over medium heat for 5 minutes. Add scampi and stir well. Add the salt, pepper, and the parsley. Cook for another 5 minutes. Remove skillet from heat and pour brandy over scampi. Remove the scampi and return the skillet to the heat. Add the whipping cream, tomato sauce and stir well. Cook for 15 minutes stirring occasionally. Add the Rice and scampi to sauce and stir well.

Comments:

Breads

Bran Brown Bread

Yields 1 large or 2 small loaves

2 tsp	sugar
1/2 cup	lukewarm water
2 tbsp	dry granular yeast
1/4 cup	shortening
1/3 cup	packed brown sugar
2 tbsp	molasses
2 tsp	salt
1 cup	milk
1 cup	water
2 cups	natural cooking bran
2 cups	all-purpose flour
3 cups	whole-wheat flour

A delicious and moist bread which may be used at any meal of the day as well as for sandwiches. Housewives used to cool their bread by leaning it against a shelf and if a crusty outside was desired they allowed the wind to blow over it as it cooled.

Dissolve the sugar in the lukewarm water and sprinkle with the yeast. Set aside to dissolve for 10 minutes. In the meantime cream together the shortening, brown sugar, molasses and salt. Add the milk, water and bran. Beat well until well blended. Stir in the yeast when dissolved. Add the all-purpose flour and gradually work in the whole-wheat flour. Turn out onto a floured board and knead for 10 to 12 minutes using as much more flour as necessary to prevent it from sticking to the board. Cover and set in a warm place to rise until doubled in bulk, approximately 1 1/2 hours. Punch down and form into one large loaf or two small loaves. Place in greased loaf pans. Let rise in a warm place until doubled, about 1/2 hour. For the large loaf bake at 375 F (190 C) for 40 to 45 minutes, or less time for smaller loaves. Cool on racks.

Comments:

Polenta

Polenta

(CORNMEAL)

Serves 6 people

Preparation Time: 20 minutes
Cooking Time: 1 hour

4 cups	water
500 grams	cornmeal (fine)
2 tbsp	salt
1/2 cup	olive oil
1/4 cup	Parmesan cheese

Bring water to a boil and add salt and oil. Slowly whisk in cornmeal and cook on low for one hour. Serve with tomato sauce and cod fish or zucchini or sausage and sprinkle cheese on top.

Comments:

Regular Bread

3 lbs	flour
1/2 litre	water
1/2 cup	sugar
3 tbsp	salt
2	eggs, beaten
3 tbsp	yeast
1/2 cup	olive oil

Mix all ingredients together and mix for one hour or more until the dough is shiny. Let rise for 4 hours. Shape into small rolls and let rise for one hour again. Bake at 350 F for one hour (you may reduce heat to 325 F after first half hour).

Comments:

Corn Bread

2 cups	cornmeal
1 cup	corn flour
1 cup	rice flour
3	eggs
1/3 cup	cooking oil
1/2 tsp	salt
1 tsp	baking soda
2 tsp	baking powder
2 1/4 cups	buttermilk

Mix ingredients together. Bake in waxed paper lined 9 x 9 inch cake pan at 350 F for 45 minutes. Test for doneness before taking out from oven. Warm 45 seconds in microwave before serving.

Comments:

Cheese

Popular Cheeses used in Classic Italian Cooking

Provolone Picante

Romano

Provoletto

Caciocavallo

Parmigiano

Asiaco

Corconzola

Bocconcini

Ricotta

Friulano

Pecorino

Marscarpone

Osteria de Medici
RISTORANTE

Torta Di Citro

(LIME CAKE)

Serves 12 people

Preparation Time: 10 minutes
Cooking Time: 10 minutes

Step 1

12	limes, squeezed for the juice
3	grated lime rinds
24	egg yolks
6 cups	sugar

In a double boiler whisk steadily together lime juice, egg yolks and sugar for 10 minutes.

Step 2

3 cups	hot milk
3 tbsp	gelatin
4 cups	32% whipping cream

Add remaining ingredients and whisk for an additional 5 minutes. Place in a round cake pan and refrigerate for 4 hours.

Comments:

Fragole Al Pepe Verde

(STRAWBERRIES WITH GREEN PEPPERCORNS)

Serves 4 people

Preparation Time: 5 minutes
Cooking Time: 5 minutes

1 lb	strawberries
1 tsp	green peppercorns
2 tbsp	butter
1 cup	sugar
1/2 cup	marsala wine
1	juice of a lemon

Clean and halve strawberries. In a saucepan melt butter and add sugar. Place strawberries and peppercorns in the saucepan. Cook for about one minute, add lemon juice and marsala wine. Continue cooking for approximately 3 more minutes. Then serve over ice cream.

Comments:

Ciliege Al Vino Rosso

(BAKED CHERRIES WITH RED WINE)

Serves 4 people

1 lb	ripe cherries
1 1/2 cup	red wine
1 tbsp	sugar
1/2 tbsp	icing sugar
1 tbsp	brandy

Place cherries in a baking dish with sugar, brandy and wine. Bake in a 350 F oven for 45 minutes. Then remove cherries and place liquid in a saucepan and cook until reduced by half. Pour sauce over cherries and let cool for approximately 1 hour prior to serving.

Comments:

Tiramisu

Serves 6 people

Preparation Time: 1 hour

8	egg yolks
2 cups	sugar
2 cups	mascarpone cheese
24 – 30	lady finger biscuits
1 litre	espresso, cold
1/2 cup	sambuca
1/2 cup	marsala
1/2 cup	amaretto

Whip egg yolks and sugar on high speed for 1/2 hour. Then add Mascarpone and one cup of cold espresso. Continue mixing for an additional 5 minutes. Mix remaining espresso with liqueur. Then dip lady fingers in coffee mixture and place one layer on the bottom of the pan. Take half of the egg mixture and place evenly on the top of the cookies. Layer remaining dipped cookies and add the rest of the egg mixture on top and spread out evenly. Refrigerate overnite.

Comments:

Torta Di Mele

(APPLE CAKE)

Serves 12 people

Preparation Time: 30 minutes
Cooking Time: 1 hour

12	eggs
2 cups	sugar
3 cups	all purpose flour
2 tsp	baking powder
1/2 cup	oil
4 medium	apples (peeled, cored and diced small)

Whip eggs, sugar and oil on high speed until peaks form, then slowly blend in flour and baking powder into egg mixture. Add apples. Preheat oven to 350 F. Place mix in a greased bun pan and bake for 20–45 minutes or until cooked inside. Let cool, then remove it from pan.

Comments:

Aranci Positano

(ORANGE COCKTAIL)

Serves 4 people

Preparation Time: 15 minutes
Cooking Time: 15 minutes

1 tbsp	butter
1/4 cup	sugar
1/4 cup	orange peel sliced thin
1 cup	freshly squeezed orange juice
4 oz	orange liqueur
2 tsp	baking soda
4	medium oranges, peeled and halved

In a medium skillet melt butter. Add sugar and orange peel and cook until brown in colour. Add orange juice, baking soda and liqueur mixing well. Cook on medium heat until sauce thickens and becomes smooth (about 6 minutes). Add orange halves and continue cooking for about 3 minutes. When ready to serve, place the orange halves in sherbert glasses and pour sauce over top.

Comments:

Macedonia Di Frutta Fresca

(FRESH FRUIT SALAD)

Serves 4 people   *Preparation Time: 20 minutes*

1	grapefruit
1	banana
2	ripe pears
1	apple
1	orange
1/2	cantaloupe
10	seedless white or red grapes
1/2	lemon, squeezed for the juice
3 tbsp	sugar
2 oz	maraschino liqueur

Wash fruit, peel and core. Cut into bite sized pieces and put in a large bowl. Squeeze lemon the juice of 1/2 lemon over the top then add the sugar and liqueur. Stir well. Cover and refrigerate for 2 hours, stirring several times.

Comments:

Ciambellone

(ITALIAN POUND CAKE)

1 cake

Preparation Time: 20 minutes
Cooking Time: 1 hour

7	eggs
1 cup	water
1/2 cup	olive oil
1 1/2 cup	sugar
3 tbsp	baking powder
2 cup	flour
1/2 cup	chopped orange peel

Beat eggs, water, oil and sugar on high for approximately 15 minutes, then fold in flour, baking powder and orange peel. Pour into a greased bread pan and bake for 1 hour at 350 F.

Comments:

Zabaglione

(HOT WHIPPED CUSTARD)

Serves 6 people

Preparation Time: 5 minutes
Cooking Time: 5 minutes

3	egg yolks
1/2 cup	sweet marsala wine
1/2 cup	dry white wine
3 tbsp	sugar

In a saucepan, bring water to a boil over medium heat. In a stainless steel bowl, place egg yolks, marsala wine, white wine and sugar. Place bowl in the saucepan. Slightly tip the bowl toward you and beat the egg mixture with a wire whisk in a backward and forward motion. Whisk constantly until egg yolks become slightly thickened and light in colour. Pour Zabaglione into champagne glasses and serve.

Comments:

Fragole Semifreddo

(STRAWBERRY PARFAIT)

Serves 2 people

1 cup	cut strawberries
1 cup	whipping cream
4	egg yolks
2 tbsp	sugar
2 tsp	kirsch
2 tsp	water

Cook strawberries in water, kirsch and 1 tbsp. of sugar for 5 minutes and let cool in the refrigerator. Whip cream on high speed until it forms peaks and refrigerate. Add 1 tbsp. of sugar. Then whip the egg yolks on high speed. Fold in whipping cream, strawberries and liquid. Place mixture in parfait glasses and freeze for 4 hours. Serve frozen.

Comments:

Banana Fritters

Serves 2 – 4 people

Preparation Time: 5 minutes
Cooking Time: 5 minutes

1 cup	flour
1 tsp	baking powder
1/2 tsp	salt
1/2 – 3/4	cup milk
1	egg, well beaten
1 tbsp	rum
1 or 2	ripe bananas
1/2 cup	sugar

Sift flour, baking powder and salt. Add milk and egg. Beat well. Skin and cut bananas in half lengthwise, then across, making 4 pieces. Drop the bananas into the batter and lift out with a fork (do not pierce). Fry in hot deep fat and drain well when nicely browned. Sprinkle liberally with sugar and rum.

Comments:

Pere Al'Amaretto

(AMARETTO PEARS)

Serves 6 people

Part A: Sauce

2 cups	sugar
1 cup	warm water
2 cups	cold water
1 cup	amaretto liqueur

Part B: Pears

4 cups	water
1/2	lemon
1	clove
2	bay leaves
6	pears, peeled, halved, and cored
1/2 cup	sugar

Combine sugar and warm water in a saucepan and bring to a boil. Stir constantly until the mixture turns a caramel colour. Remove from heat. Slowly stir in cold water and amaretto liqueur. Return it to the heat and simmer until the sauce has reduced and thickens (about 10 minutes). Remove from heat and cool. Place in the refrigerator.

In a saucepan, combine bay leaves, clove and lemon to 4 cups of water. Bring to a boil. Add the pears and sugar. Stir and simmer for one half hour over heat. Then let pears cool in the water. When cool, drain and place in sherbet glasses and pour the sauce over top.

Comments:

Creme Caramel

(CARAMEL CUSTARD)

Serves 4 people

Preparation Time: 5 minutes
Cooking Time: 30 – 35 minutes

Part A: Sauce

2 cups	sugar
1 cup	water

In a saucepan combine sugar and water. Bring to a boil stirring constantly until the mixture turns to a caramel colour. Remove from heat and pour sauce evenly into 4 custard cups. Refrigerate for 20 minutes or until the sauce has hardened.

Part B: Custard

1/3 cup	galliano liqueur
4	eggs
1/4 cup	sugar
2 cups	warm milk

Preheat oven to 350 F. In a medium bowl, beat eggs. Add sugar, milk and liqueur, mixing well. Set aside. Remove the custard cups from the refrigerator and evenly divide the egg mixture into each of the cups. Set custard cups in a pan of water about half the depth of the custard. Bake for 1/2 an hour. Custard is done when it feels firm to the touch. Remove the custard from the oven and chill custard cups in the refrigerator. Invert on a plate. Serve chilled.

Comments:

Soufflé

Osteria de Medici
RISTORANTE

Soufflé au Grand Marnier

(ORANGE LIQUEUR SOUFFLÉ)

Serves 4 people

2 tbsp	soft butter
3 tbsp	sugar
5	egg yolks
1/3 cup	sugar
1/4 cup	Grand Marnier (1 two-ounce bottle)
1 tbsp	freshly grated orange peel
7	egg whites
1/4 tsp	cream of tartar
	confectioners' (powdered) sugar

Preheat the oven to 425 F. Grease the bottom and sides of a 1 1/2 quart soufflé dish with 2 tablespoons of soft butter. Sprinkle in 3 tablespoons of sugar, tipping and shaking the dish to spread the sugar evenly. Then turn the dish over and knock out the excess sugar. Set aside. In the top of a double boiler, beat the egg yolks with a whisk, rotary or electric beater until they are well blended. Slowly add the sugar and continue beating until the yolks become very thick and pale yellow. Set the pan over barely simmering (not boiling) water and heat the egg yolks, stirring gently and constantly with a wooden spoon or rubber spatula, until the mixture thickens and becomes almost too hot to touch. Stir in the Grand Marnier and grated orange peel and transfer to a large bowl. Set the bowl into a pan filled with crushed ice or ice cubes and cold water, and stir the mixture until it is quite cold. Remove it from the ice. In a large mixing bowl, preferably of unlined copper, beat the egg whites and the cream of tartar with a clean whisk or rotary beater until they form stiff, unwavering peaks. Using a rubber spatula, stir a large spoonful of beaten egg white into the egg-yolk mixture to lighten it. Gently fold the remaining egg whites into the mixture. Spoon the soufflé into the buttered, sugared dish, filling it to within 2 inches of the top. Smooth the top of the soufflé with the spatula. For a decorative effect, make a cap on the soufflé by cutting a trench about 1 inch deep 1 inch from the edge all around the top.

Bake on the middle shelf of the oven for 2 minutes, then reduce the heat to 400 F. Continue baking for another 20 to 30 minutes, or until the soufflé has risen about 2 inches above the top of the mold and the top is lightly browned. Sprinkle with confectioners' sugar and serve it at once.

Comments:

Gelati

(VANILLA ICE CREAM)

To make about 1 1/2 pints

2 cups	light cream
2 inch	piece of vanilla bean
or	
1 tsp	vanilla extract
8	egg yolks
1/2 cup	sugar
1 cup	heavy cream

In a 1 1/2 or 2 quart enameled or stainless-steel saucepan, bring the light cream and the vanilla bean almost to a boil over low heat. (If you are using vanilla extract, do not add it now.) Meanwhile combine the egg yolks and sugar in a bowl. Beat them with a whisk, rotary or electric beater for 3 to 5 minutes, or until they are pale yellow and thick enough to fall from the whisk or beater in a lazy ribbon. Then discard the vanilla bean from the saucepan and pour the hot cream slowly into the beaten egg yolks, beating gently and constantly. Pour the mixture back into the saucepan and cook over moderately low heat, stirring constantly with a wooden spoon, until it thickens to a custard that lightly coats the spoon. Do not allow the mixture to boil or it will curdle. Stir in the heavy cream, and if you are using the vanilla extract instead of the vanilla bean, add it now. Strain the custard through a fine sieve into a mixing bowl and allow it to cool to room temperature.

Now pack a 2 quart ice cream freezer with layers of finely crushed or cracked ice and coarse rock salt in the proportions recommended by the freezer manufacturer. Add cold water if the manufacturer advises it. Then pour or ladle the cooled gelato into the ice cream can and cover it. If you have a hand ice cream maker let it stand for 3 to 4 minutes before turning the handle. It may take 15 minutes or more for the ice cream to freeze, but do not stop turning at any time, or the gelato may be lumpy. When the handle can barely be moved, the ice cream should be firm. If you have an electric ice cream maker, turn it on and let it churn for about 15 minutes, or until the motor slows or actually stops.

To harden the gelato, scrape the ice cream from the sides down into the bottom of the can and cover it very securely. Drain off any water that is in the bucket and repack it with ice and salt. Let it stand for 2 to 3 hours.

Comments:

Pistachio Ice Cream

To make about 1 1/2 pints

2 cups	light cream
8	egg yolks
6 tbsp	sugar
2 1/2 tbsp	ground or crushed shelled pistachio nuts
1 cup	heavy cream
7 drops	green food colouring
5 1/2 tbsp	chopped shelled pistachio nuts
1/4 cup	ground blanched almonds

Heat the light cream and beat the egg yolks and sugar together. Add the ground pistachio nuts and make the custard as in Gelati recipe. Then stir in the heavy cream and vegetable colouring and strain this mixture. Add the chopped pistachio nuts and ground almonds. Cool and freeze.

Comments:

Coffee Ice Cream

To make about 1 1/2 pints

2 cups	light cream
2 inch	strip of fresh lemon peel
8	egg yolks
6 tbsp	sugar
2 tbsp	espresso coffee
2 cups	heavy cream

Heat the light cream with the lemon peel and beat the egg yolks and sugar together. Discard the peel and make the custard as in Gelati recipe. Add the espresso coffee (instant or freshly brewed) and heavy cream; strain, cool and freeze.

Comments:

Chocolate Ice Cream

To make about 1 1/2 pints

2 cups	milk
4	egg yolks
10 tbsp	sugar
2 cups	heavy cream
4 oz	semisweet chocolate, melted
1/2 tsp	vanilla extract

Heat the milk, beat the egg yolks and sugar together, and make the custard as in Gelati recipe. Then stir in the heavy cream, melted chocolate and vanilla extract. Strain, cook and freeze.

Comments:

Cassata all Siciliana

Serves 8

A fresh pound cake about 9 inches long
and 3 inches wide

1 lb	ricotta cheese
2 tbsp	heavy cream
1/4 cup	sugar
3 tbsp	Strega or other orange flavoured liqueur
3 tbsp	coarsely chopped mixed candied fruit
2 oz	semisweet chocolate, coarsely chopped

With a sharp, serrated knife, slice the end crusts off the pound cake and level the top if it is rounded. Cut the cake horizontally into 1/2 to 3/4 inch thick slabs. Rub the ricotta through a coarse sieve into a bowl with a wooden spoon and beat it with a rotary or electric beater until it is smooth. Beating constantly, add the cream, sugar and Strega. With a rubber spatula, fold in the chopped candied fruit and chocolate. Center the bottom slab of the cake on a flat plate and spread it generously with the ricotta mixture. Carefully place another slab of cake on top, keeping sides and ends even, and spread with more ricotta. Repeat until all the cake slabs are reassembled and the filling has been used up — ending with a plain slice of cake on top. Gently press the loaf together to make it as compact as possible. Do not worry if it feels wobbly; chilling firms the loaf. Refrigerate the cassata for about 2 hours, or until the ricotta is firm.

Chocolate Frosting

12 oz	semisweet chocolate, cut in small pieces
3/4 cup	strong black coffee
1/2 lb	unsalted butter, cut into 1/2 inch pieces and thoroughly chilled

Melt 12 ounces of chocolate with the coffee in a small heavy saucepan over low heat, stirring constantly until the chocolate has completely dissolved. Remove the pan from the heat and beat in the chilled butter, 1 piece at a time. Continue beating until the mixture is smooth. Then chill this frosting until it thickens to spreading consistency. With a small metal spatula, spread the frosting evenly over the top, sides and ends of the cassata, swirling it as decoratively as you can. Cover loosely with plastic wrap, wax paper or aluminum foil and let the cassata "ripen" in the refrigerator for at least 24 hours before serving it.

Comments:

Granite

(FLAVOURED ICES)

To make about 1 1/2 pints of each flavor

Lemon Ice

2 cups	water
1 cup	sugar
1 cup	lemon juice

Orange Ice

2 cups	water
3/4 cup	sugar
1 cup	orange juice
	juice of 1 lemon

Coffee Ice

1 cup	water
1/2 cup	sugar
2 cups	strong espresso coffee

Strawberry Ice

1 cup	water
1/2 cup	sugar
2 cups	fresh ripe strawberries, pureed through sieve
2 tbsp	lemon juice

In a 1 1/2 to 2 quart saucepan, bring the water and sugar to a boil over moderate heat, stirring only until the sugar dissolves. Timing from the moment the sugar and water begin to boil, let the mixture cook for exactly 5 minutes. Immediately remove the pan from the heat and let the syrup cool to room temperature.

Depending on which of the flavoured ices you want to make, stir in the lemon juice, or the orange and lemon juices, or espresso coffee, or the pureed strawberries and lemon juice. Pour the mixture into an ice–cube tray from which the divider has been removed.

Freeze the granita for 3 to 4 hours, stirring it every 30 minutes and scraping into it the ice particles that form around the edges of the tray. The finished granita should have a fine, snowy texture. For a coarser texture that is actually more the Italian taste, leave the ice cube divider in the tray and freeze the granita solid. Then remove the cubes and crush them in an ice crusher.

Note: if you use frozen strawberries rather than fresh ones, make the syrup with only 1/4 cup of sugar.

Comments:

Let us not forget the babies, following are a few recipes for the young ones. Each recipe calls for the freshest produce and meats. After all, babies are as important as adults.

Pastina in Brodo

(SMALL PASTAS IN BROTH)

Serves 1 baby

Preparation Time: 5 minutes
Cooking Time: 15 minutes

1 cup	pastina
2 cups	chicken broth
	salt to taste

Cook pasta in a large amount of salted boiling water. Meanwhile bring broth to a boil and add salt. Strain Pastina and add to the broth.

Comments:

Zucchini Con Riso Bodino

(ZUCCHINI AND RICE PUREE)

Serves 1 baby

Preparation Time: 5 minutes
Cooking Time: 1 hour

1/2 cup	rice
1/4	fresh tomato
1/2	zucchini, small
2 cups	chicken broth
	salt to taste

Cook rice separately in 2 cups of water until the rice is cooked and all the liquid has evaporated. Bring broth to a boil, add zucchini and tomato. Cook until the vegetables are soft. Add cooked rice and puree in a food processor.

Comments:

Bodino Di Pollo

(CREAMED CHICKEN)

Serves 1 baby

Preparation Time: 5 minutes
Cooking Time: 1 hour

1/2	chicken breast
1/2	medium potato, peeled
1/2	celery stalk
1/2	carrot
1/4	onion
2 cups	water
1 tsp	salt
2	fresh basil leaves

Place all ingredients in a small pot and bring to a boil, then simmer until vegetables are soft. Remove from pot and puree in a food processor.

Comments:

Bodino Di Mele

(PUREED APPLES)

Serves 1 baby

Preparation Time: 5 minutes
Cooking Time: 1/2 hour

1	peeled apple, cored
3 cups	water
1 tsp	sugar

Place all ingredients including skin into a pot and simmer until apple is very soft. Remove from the pot the apple and blend in a food processor. Serve cold. The skins are used when boiling because they contain the essential vitamins. Apples can be substituted by pears or peaches.

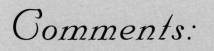

Comments:

Camomile Herb Tea

1	camomile tea bag
4 cups	hot water
	sugar to taste
	and it is ready for your young one

Canarino

1 litre	water
3 med	lemon skins
	sugar to taste
	boil for 20 minutes
	may be served hot or cold

*These drinks are also used by people who prefer caffeine-free drinks.

Comments:

Table Setting

Osteria de Medici
RISTORANTE

Special

Occasions

La Cena Di San Valentino

(ST. VALENTINE'S DINNER)

Menu

Baked Mushrooms and Scallops p. 97

Pheasant with Porcini Sauce p. 126

Zucchini Al Pomodoro p. 152

Risotto Zaferano p. 168

Fragola Semifreddo p. 194

Festa Pasquale

(EASTER FEAST)

Serves 10–12 people

Preparation Time: 30 minutes
Cooking Time: 1 1/2 hours

16 lbs	baby lamb
6	garlic cloves
1/2 cup	chopped parsley
3 tbsp	rosemary
2 cups	olive oil
3 cups	white wine
	salt and pepper to taste

Cut lamb into four pieces. Place it in a large baking pan with oil and bake for 3/4 hour at 400 F. Drain oil and add garlic, rosemary, parsley, salt and pepper. Continue cooking for 10 minutes. Add wine and cut into portions and serve with roasted potatoes and peas.

Comments:

Tacchino Ripieno

(THANKSGIVING DINNER)

Serves 8–10 people

Preparation Time: 30 minutes
Cooking Time: 4 hours

10–12 lb turkey

1 lb	chicken liver, chopped
4	eggs
1/2 cup	chopped parsley
1 med	green pepper, chopped
3 cups	parmesan cheese
3 cups	bread crumbs
4	garlic cloves, chopped
3 cups	white wine

2	carrots, chopped
1	onion, chopped

Season turkey inside and out. Then mix all stuffing ingredients in a large bowl, and stuff turkey. Rub turkey with oil and place in a 350 F oven for about 30 minutes. Then add vegetables to the pan and continue cooking for another 2 hours. Then drain grease and remove turkey. Place pan on top of the stove and turn on high, add wine and thicken with beurre manier* and season to taste. Serve with red and green peppers, green beans and potatoes.

*Refer to page 19

Comments:

Panettone

(CHRISTMAS BREAD)

Serves 12 people

Preparation Time: 30 minutes
Cooking Time: 1 hour

4 cup	flour
1 cup	softened butter
4	eggs
1 cup	milk
1 1/2 cup	sugar
1 tbsp	vanilla
1 tbsp	brandy
1 tbsp	rum
1 tbsp	grated lemon rind
1 tsp	salt
1 cup	raisins
4 tsp	baking powder
1 cup	chopped citron
1 cup	chopped maraschino cherries
1 cup	chopped walnuts

Cream butter and sugar, then add lemon rind, eggs one at a time, beating well after each. Add milk, vanilla, brandy, rum and blend well. Sift flour, baking powder and salt together and gradually add to the creamed mixture. Fold in raisins, citron, cherries and nuts until well blended. Pour into 9" angel food pan and bake at 350 F for about 1 hour. Test with a tooth pick.

Comments:

Vineyards

Wine

Regional Wine

Valbiferno – This name is used by the ancient inhabitants of the hills where the vineyards are found which produce this particular red wine. It is a ruby red colour with purple tints, and a pleasant bouquet. The flavour is refined, smooth, well balanced, easy to drink. It accompanies roasts and cheeses well.

Liburno – Wine from a hill named Liburno near the south boundary of the Sannto district. This is a white wine made from Trebbiano grapes which give it delicate flavours and bouquets. It should be drunk young at 10–12 degrees with hors d'oeuvres, fish and cold white meats.

Wine Storage

All bottles of wine should be kept lying down so that the corks remain moist to keep them from drying out and permitting air to come into contact with the contents. Air is the prime enemy of wine, and keeping the cork wet prohibits air entry into the bottle. Dessert wines are an exception to this rule. Due to their higher alcohol content, deterioration is prevented, and these wines may be stored with the neck up.

Wine

MY FATHER – NICOLA BARILE

My father taught me how to make wine. I did help my father to make wine as he was the best wine maker. Best for the month of October.

17 cases	grapes in total (each case is 42 lbs)
4 cases	moscat grapes (white)
4 cases	alleganti
3 cases	barberra
3 cases	garingani
3 cases	zinfandel
Yield:	one barrel (48 gallons)

Grind all grapes together. Let ferment in barrel for at least 6 days in a cool, dark place (20–40 F). Drain through tap or siphon into bottles.

Comments:

Traditional Italian Christmas Feast

Antipasto Di Gamberetti (Shrimp Cocktail) p. 32
Antipasto Frutti Di-Mare (Cold Seafood Appetizer) p. 27

Eve Dinner

Salmone Al Funghi (Salmon with Mushrooms) p. 106
Ciambellone (Italian Pound Cake) p. 192

Index

Index

Index

In this day and age, it is important to be able to quickly prepare good nutritious meals, that is why each one of the recipes that are in this book indicate the preparation time and the cooking time, allowing you to choose recipes that fit into your schedule.

I hope you will enjoy preparing these wonderful recipes for your family and friends as much as I do.

Have fun cooking. Love,

Osteria de Medici
RISTORANTE

Divertitevi Provando le Mie Ricette

(HAVE FUN TRYING MY RECIPES)

Buono Appetito

(ENJOY YOUR DINNER)

Please write to me once you have tried some of these receipes and let me know how they turned out.

— Antoinette

Osteria de Medici
RISTORANTE

201–10th Street N.W.
Calgary, AB
T2N 1U5

When visiting Scottsdale, Arizona please visit our sister restaurant.

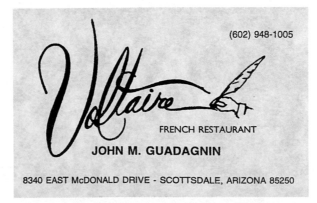

Acknowledgements

*Production Co-ordination
by Maurizio Terrigno*

Printing: Ronalds Printing, Calgary, Alberta

Additional Copies:
Available from your local bookstore or by contacting:

Osteria de Medici
RISTORANTE
*201-10th Street N.W.
Calgary, AB
T2N 1U5
Phone (403) 283-5553   Toll Free 1-888-678-3742*